9-8-59

The
Presbyterian Liturgies

The
Presbyterian Liturgies

Historical Sketches

by

Charles W. Baird

BAKER BOOK HOUSE
Grand Rapids 6, Mich.
1957

Library of Congress Catalog Card Number: 57-8257

Previously printed under the
title Chapter on Liturgies (1856)
and Eutaxia (1855)

PHOTOLITHOPRINTED BY CUSHING - MALLOY, INC.
ANN ARBOR, MICHIGAN, UNITED STATES OF AMERICA
1957

CONTENTS.

1084245

PREFACE

The liturgical sketches comprising this book were published in the year 1855 in New York. This first edition was entitled: *EUTAXIA, or the Presbyterian Liturgies;* Historical Sketches. The author was a young Presbyterian minister who preferred to remain anonymous. The title page simply stated: By a Minister of the Presbyterian Church.

Already during the year following its publication the book was republished in London, England, for the readers of the British Isles. This London edition of 1856 was introduced by the Reverend Thomas Binnie, English Congregationalist minister, and later professor of homiletics and pastoral theology at New College, London. The book now appeared with the author's name, the Reverend Charles W. Baird. This London edition bore the title: *A Chapter on Liturgy.*

I consider these sketches by Baird to be very valuable, and I was happy to learn that the Baker

Book House was ready to place a reprint of this liturgical gem on the market. I am persuaded that in republishing this book the publishers are rendering us a genuine service. For these sketches are among the best regarding the liturgy of the churches belonging to the Reformed, Presbyterian wing of the reformation. I heartily recommend the study of this volume to all who love God's Church, and desire to see the Church's worship services built and developed according to Scriptural principles.

The present reprint is based on the 1856 London edition, for which edition Baird himself made some minor improvements and added the fourfold supplement. The publishers, however, wisely confined the present volume to that which the Reverend Baird himself wrote. This means that the rather lengthy introduction, and a concluding chapter on liturgical problems, both written by Professor Binnie, have been omitted. This was done inasmuch as these contributions were written very definitely with the readers and the ecclesiastical situation of Great Britain of 100 years ago in mind.

May God command His blessing upon the present republication of this worthy volume.

MARTIN MONSMA
Professor, Practical Theology,
Calvin Seminary, Grand Rapids, Michigan

A

CHAPTER ON LITURGIES.

Introduction.

"If the Parson were ashamed of particularizing in these things, he were not fit to be a Parson; but he holds the Rule, that *Nothing is little in God's Service:* If it once have the honour of that Name, it grows great instantly."—THE COUNTRY PARSON, ch. xiv.

To ascertain from the history and teachings of the Presbyterian Church, what may be considered the proper theory of its worship, and to compare that ideal with our prevailing practice, is my purpose in the following researches. I have chosen for their title a term compendiously designating that due observance of decorum, and regard to comeliness of word and action, which in the public service of GOD I seek with all humility to advocate. Generically, the term is no other than that used by the Apostle, in his command, "Let all things be done decently and in order;"* a

* 1 Cor. xiv. 40.—Εὐσχημόνως καὶ κατὰ τάξιν. See, in relation to this passage and note, the Preface by the Editor.

B

precept affording sufficient warrant for the discussion upon which I have presumed to enter.

The scriptural idea of public worship is clearly that of a service *prescribed* as to its several component parts, but *free* in the filling up of its general outlines. The observance of the LORD's Day by attendance upon religious ministrations; participation in the sacraments; the singing of psalms, and hymns, and spiritual songs; the reading of Scripture; and the making of supplications, prayers, intercessions, and thanksgiving: these are all matters of direct Divine appointment. But apart from these, there are considerations of propriety and taste, as to the form and manner of discharging the required duties: which, although important and worthy of careful attention, the Apostles seem to have left, with a few general directions like that given to the Corinthian Church, for individual or ecclesiastical adjustment; considerations of comeliness and decorum, appropriately to be settled in accordance with the peculiar circumstances under which they might severally come up. To this category belongs, unquestionably, the subject of the choice of language to be used in the services of public devotion.

It has been the wisdom of the Presbyterian

Church to follow strictly this scriptural and Apostolic method; imposing as duties, only such acts and ordinances of worship as are of Divine appointment; and leaving in a great measure to individual choice the selection of words employed in their performance. The Directory of Worship, set forth by the Assembly at Westminster, and adopted by our Mother Church as one of her standards, contains such regulations, referring to all the parts of Divine service; minutely and definitely prescribing the topics of prayer, their sequence and proportions; in fact, embracing all the themes of worship, without rigid confinement to set words and phrases. This Directory, the laborious production of the ablest divines of the period, is all that our Church has enjoined as a matter of strict requisition upon her ministers and people; leaving entire liberty in respect to the language that shall embody and express these prescribed topics. But it is quite evident, at the same time, that however this Directory of Worship may meet the aim of our Church in regard to the performance of religious rites, and exactly correspond with inspired precept and primitive practice, it does not meet all the wants of public devotion, nor answer all the ends of an aid to public prayer. It defines

and arranges the parts of Divine service; but it
does not furnish forms of language suitable for
their expression. The need of assistance to the
minister in conducting, and to the people in
following oral supplications, is not supplied by a
work whose whole object is to state and describe
the constituent elements of worship. There is a
necessity palpable and widely felt, for something
more than this, to meet the exigencies of the case.

Does the Presbyterian Church allow or contemplate any such subsidiary provision for the
celebration of public worship? Are her ministers
precluded from the use of sound and well-conceived formularies, and shut up to the necessity
of original composition for this most solemn, difficult, and trying function of their office, without
even the right of previous preparation for the
task? There is in the Church of CHRIST a rich
and copious literature of devotion, accumulated
by the labours of many ages. Holy men of prayer
have been gifted at some periods, as few can claim
to be now, with elevation of thought and language
necessary for the adequate expression of devout
feeling. The period of primitive zeal produced
such minds. The period of reformation in the
Church brought out others. Are we, in less

favoured days, debarred from the fruits of these high spiritual endowments? Do our ecclesiastical rules exclude us from the use of the best liturgical compositions, and force us to rely on our individual resources of conception, however crude, and meagre, and immature we may find them?

Such is undoubtedly the popular conception of the matter; and the fact of its general, if not universal prevalence, has led me to attempt an exhibition of the true theory, and the normal practice of our Church in this particular. It will be my object to demonstrate, first, *That the principles of Presbyterianism in no wise conflict with the discretionary use of written forms;* and, secondly, *That the practice of Presbyterian churches abundantly warrants the adoption and the use of such forms.*

The principles of our Church, in regard to public worship, are easily gathered from her standards, and from the opinions of those who are considered their ablest and most authentic exponents. It might be inferred, from the common notion of her antipathy to all preconceived forms, that our Church expressly and strongly condemns their use. No such prohibition occurs in her standards. There is rather a studious avoidance of anything like this condemnation; resembling the tone of one who cautiously refrains from censuring her own past action, however it may differ from her present habits.

The Directory of Worship reprobates, indeed, the "*confining*" of ministers to set or fixed forms; but, far from discouraging preparation, it recommends the "reading of the best writers on the subject." The language of our theologians is yet more clear and unmistakeable: "We are very far from pronouncing, or even thinking," says a venerated divine, recently deceased, "that it is unlawful to conduct prayer, either public or private, by a form. We should deem such a sentence or opinion altogether erroneous. There is no reason to doubt that many a truly fervent and acceptable prayer has been offered in this manner. Some of the most excellent men that ever adorned the Church of CHRIST have decisively preferred this method of conducting the devotions of the sanctuary, and have no doubt found it compatible with the most exalted spirit of prayer. We only contend that such forms are not indispensable, as some contend, to orderly and edifying prayer. . . . And that to *impose* forms of prayer at all times, and upon all persons who publicly minister in holy things, and to *confine* them to the use of such forms, is by no means either desirable or wise."*

From another and equally authoritative source, I gained a similar opinion: "*Not condemning* either the principle or use of a Liturgy, the Presbyterian Church, nevertheless, from a conviction that the practice of *confining* ministers to set or fixed forms of prayers for public worship, derives no warrant from the spirit and examples of the word of GOD, nor from the practice of the Primitive Church, and that it is, moreover, unprofitable, burdensome to Christian liberty, and otherwise inexpedient,—disapproves of such restrictions; but she has, at the same time, made such provisions in her 'Directory' for the service, that it may be performed with dignity and propriety, as well as profit, to those who join in it, and that it may not be disgraced by mean, irregular, or extravagant effusions." †

As it respects the existence of authorized forms

* The Rev. SAMUEL MILLER, D.D., late Professor of Ecclesiastical History in the Theological Seminary of the Presbyterian Church, in his work on "*Public Prayer*," pp. 138, 139.

† Rev. JOHN M. KREBS, D.D., Permanent Clerk of the General Assembly of the Presbyterian Church, in an article contributed to a "*History of the Religious Denominations in the United States*, by J. D. Rupp." Philad., 1844: pp. 564—566.

of worship in the Presbyterian Church, it will be my aim to show, that the idea of a Liturgy has not been foreign to our system; that forms of this nature have, at various periods, been drawn up and used; that previous to the date of the Westminster Assembly, there prevailed in Scotland an order of worship liturgical in its character, which, indeed, has never been officially abrogated; and that the authorship of those forms is to be ascribed to no meaner sources than our own great Reformers, Knox and Calvin, the founders of modern Presbyterianism.

And here let me define the meaning of the term "Liturgy" when used in a Presbyterian sense. The churches of the Reformation have treated the subject of public worship according to four different methods.

The first is that of an *imposed* ritual, responsive in its character, and prescribed to the minister and people for their common use. Such is the practice of the Anglican and Lutheran communions.

Another method is that of a *discretionary* ritual, not responsive, and supplied to the minister alone,*

* In France and Switzerland, but few copies of the Liturgies in use are printed, and these are to be procured, as a general thing, only by ministers.

for his guidance as to the matter and manner of worship; leaving freedom of variation, as to the latter, according to his judgment.   Such was the usage of the Church of Scotland, for the first century of her existence; such is the practice of every Reformed Church on the Continent of Europe at the present time; and such was the plan proposed by Rodgers, Green, and other of our American divines, at the period of the organization of our Church in this country.

The third method is that of a *rubrical* provision; consisting of directions without examples; indicating the subjects, but omitting the language of prayer.   Of this character was the Directory composed by the Westminster Assembly, and adopted by our Church.

And the fourth method, if such we may call it, is that of *entire freedom*, as respects both subject and language; leaving all to the option of the minister.   Perhaps no denomination has followed this course, since the days of the old Independents, who opposed even the introduction of a Directory of Worship, as hampering the liberty of the individual.*

* HETHERINGTON'S *History of the Westminster Assembly of Divines*, ch. iii.   NEALE'S *History of the Puritans*, vol. ii.   The same

It is only the second and third of the four methods here indicated that will be embraced by our remarks; those usages between which the practice of our own Church has been divided: the former being her ancient custom, the latter the more modern. Be it understood that where occasion leads us to allude to the comparative merits of liturgical and rubrical forms, we shall speak only of those two methods which have been equally approved, honoured, and practised in our own Church. We have nothing to do, by way of recommending or denouncing, with the first of these methods—an imposed, prescriptive Liturgy, admitting of no variation. Our Church knows nothing of such custom, and it will therefore fall outside of the range of our observations.

There exists among us a strong and justifiable feeling, which I would be the last to weaken, opposed to the borrowing of forms and ceremonies alien from our ecclesiastical spirit. The dignity of our Church, to say nothing of individual self-respect, would suffer by such an imitation. We may not censure the practices of other commu-

view was taken by MILTON, whose dislike for Presbyterianism was almost as marked as his hatred of Prelacy. See the "*Answer to Eikon Basilike*," c. xvi.

nions; yet the fact that they are heterogeneous to our own system forbids their introduction. The spirit of Jenny Geddes is yet alive, and would be apt to resent no less resolutely, though doubtless in a fashion more accordant with the times, the attempt to foist strange ceremonies upon our simple worship. But if, on the other hand, it should appear reasonable to hope that those wants which are deeply felt and widely acknowledged among us, in regard to the public services of our churches at the present day, may be supplied by a return to our own ancient and venerable customs; by a resumption of that which has been long forsaken, yet remains admirable and excellent still:—Are we asking too much when we claim for these heir-looms of the past a careful and candid consideration?

"The ministers and members of the Presbyterian Church," says a late excellent writer, "have reason to be thankful that they belong to a body which is not restrained by any secular power from making such improvements in their system of worship as the word of GOD and more ample experience may dictate. . . . Whatever is most agreeable to the word of GOD, and most edifying to the Body of CHRIST, we are, happily, at full liberty to introduce, and progressively to modify."*

There are favoured spirits, to whom the want of help in the language of devotion is unknown. Endowed with a spiritual fluency, akin to the free utterance of a disembodied state, they pour forth in unpremeditated strain

"The gushing thoughts that struggle to have way."

These are the gifted sons of the Church: for them nothing herein contained is meant. Let them pass by, without rebuke, the means which they do not require; charitably conceding, that there may be sincerity among less fortunate worshippers, whose unready thought and slow speech justify them in borrowing suggestions and expressions from others.

But whether available or not, for present adoption and use, we think it clear beyond question, that the documents here gathered for the first time, are worthy of careful preservation; that the facts which relate to the authorship and history of these ancient formularies, have their importance, and claim a place in the records of the

* MILLER *on Public Prayer*, p. 40.

Presbyterian Church. It is surely time that these materials, so long buried in oblivion, should be sought after, and brought forth to the view of men. It is time that the radicalism which had abandoned to utter neglect these Institutes of Divine worship, should be silenced by the authoritative voice of those great reformers, who have long been represented as the advocates of this abuse. To see this justice rendered, will be an ample reward for the researches which have produced this compilation.

I.

Calvin and the Church of Geneva.

"Inward truth of heart alone, is what the LORD requires. Exercises superadded are to be approved, so far as they are subservient to Truth, useful incitements, or marks of profession to attest our faith to men. Nor do we reject things tending to the preservation of Order and Discipline. But when consciences are put under fetters, and bound by religious obligations, in matters in which GOD willed them to be free, then we must boldly protest in order that the worship of GOD be not vitiated by human fictions."—CALVIN.

GENEVA was already free from the burden of the Romish ceremonial, when Calvin came to take up his abode in that city. This fact must be borne in mind, while we endeavour to appreciate the labours of that Reformer, in reconstructing the worship of his Church. A more impetuous champion of the cause had preceded him, sweeping away every vestige of superstition, with much besides that was indifferent and harmless, from the service and the garniture of the churches. The arrangement was doubtless providential. Before Calvin could build up the Christian edifice, Farel was needed to pull down the altars of idolatry.

William Farel was the iconoclast of the Swiss Reformation. Already had he performed a task of Augean purification in several towns of the Republic, displaying energy and intrepidity such as no opposition could withstand. Thus at Neufchatel, in the course of a few days he removed every trace of the offensive ritual, drove away or brought over all the priests, and converted or silenced the masses of the population. Having thoroughly purged the Cathedral of that city from all Romish adornments, and substituted for the high altar two tables of communion, he placed upon them the bread and wine of the sacrament; and then mounting a pulpit, exclaimed to his astonished audience, as he pointed to the transformation: "This is the service your Father requires, that you should worship Him in spirit and in truth; for the Father seeketh of you none other worship than this."*

At Aigle, at Lausanne, this fearless preacher of the gospel accomplished a similar work. The turn of Geneva came at length. That city, notorious for dissoluteness of manners and superstition of creed, overrun with priests and nuns,

* LE CHRONIQUEUR, *Recueil historique*, 1535, 1536. Lausanne, 1836, p. 144.

crowded with taverns, resounding with merriment and debauch, was to become the residence of grave and severe reformers, the capital of Protestant Europe, a model of order and virtue for the world.

The Reformation at Geneva had spread widely among the people, before its magistrates could be persuaded to yield to the movement. Farel, for some months after his arrival, was refused permission to preach in the more important churches, and was obliged to hold his meetings in a suburb of the town. But on the 8th of August, 1535, impatient at the delay of their magistrates, the people assembled in great numbers at the Cathedral, rang the bells, and sent for the preacher of the Gospel. Farel came, nothing loth, ascended the pulpit, and preached. It was the first triumph of the Reformation in Geneva. No sooner did this audacious act come to the ears of the magistrates, than they summoned the offender before them. When asked how he dared to occupy that pulpit contrary to the injunction of the authorities, Farel answered, with a bold countenance: "I am astonished that you should put such a question to me. Know you not, that what I did was a holy duty, acceptable to GOD and agreeable to his

Gospel?" The magistrates, embarrassed by such a reply, remanded the preacher to appear before them on the following day.

But meanwhile, a band of little children were bringing to naught the counsels of the wise. While the priests at St. Peter's were engaged at vespers in singing the hundred and fourteenth Psalm, *in Exitu Israël,* these children, of their own accord, set up an outcry of shouts and screams to mimic the chanting of the priests. A few Protestants who were present caught the idea, and, rushing with these young reformers into the choir, broke down the altar and the images, and dispersed the officiating priests. " The children," says an old chronicler, " began to run and skip about, carrying these little idols in their arms, and crying out with joyous voices to the people who had gathered in front of the church, ' We have got the gods of the priests ; will you have some ?' And they threw them after the passers-by."*

Farel, with his fellow-labourers, was now free to proclaim the Gospel, and institute the pure worship of GOD. But the religious services which

* LE CHRONIQUEUR, etc., p. 135. See, also, an interesting volume of sketches entitled, FAREL, FROMENT, VIRET, by CHENE-VIERE : Geneva, 1835, p. 192.

they proceeded to establish were of the most plain and bald simplicity. Preaching was almost the only function performed in the churches. Sermons were delivered in abundance: on week-days, at six in the morning; on Sundays, at four, "for the convenience of servants," and twice again in the course of the day. Attendance on these services was made compulsory, and fines were imposed on such as absented themselves from church.*

Geneva thus far had neither Confession of Faith nor Order of Worship. Farel was not the man to supply this want. All that he did towards the performance of Divine service, was to set the Apostles' Creed and Ten Commandments to music, and cause them to be sung by the congregation. At the beginning of his sermons he was in the habit of pronouncing the LORD's Prayer, and some-times a brief extemporaneous supplication. But

---

* *Extraits des Registres du Conseil d'Etat;* quoted in *Le Jubilé de la Réformation.* Geneva, 1835, p. 244.

"The 8th September [1535], Master William Farel entered, and made a remonstrance, giving a written notice, whereupon it was determined, that because the writings of the said William are so godly, there shall be preaching at six in the morning at the Church of St. Germain, whither the Councillors shall be obliged to come, in order that they may repair at seven o'clock to the Council. It was also determined that J. Balard be sent for; and should he refuse to go to hear preaching, that he be imprisoned, and conducted every day to hear it. It was likewise resolved that the same thing be done in regard to all others."

as yet neither psalm-book nor liturgy assisted the devotions of the faithful.

When, therefore, in 1536, Calvin came to the city of his adoption, he found the way clear to inaugurate a pure, solemn, and scriptural mode of worship, such as might be deduced from the doctrine of revelation and the example of Apostolic times. In fact, no other course was practicable but such a return to primitive usage. Nothing remained of the Romish ritual to correct and improve. All had been abolished that might otherwise have served as the framework of an expurgated service. Popular prejudice was ready to assail the slightest appearance of a resumption of repudiated forms. The moderation which was so striking a feature of Calvin's character, might have led him to retain many excellencies of the ancient worship, omitting only what was corrupt and useless. We have reason to believe that such would have been his natural course. That he could discriminate impartially between the substance and the superadditions of many of the Romish practices, is clear to any student of his writings.* But the case would not allow such

---

* Thus we find him favourable to the rite of confirmation. " We should like," he says, " to see that rite everywhere restored by which

discrimination, and the course which he adopted was obviously, under the circumstances, most wise and prudent.

The ritual of Calvinism, like its creed, was founded, therefore, on the theory of a simple return to the scriptural and primitive pattern. Differing from the systems of Luther and Cranmer, it lost sight completely of all practices which had originated in a less remote antiquity; it left the missal and the breviary among the rubbish of "idolatrous gear" swept out from its renovated churches; refusing to tamper with the complications of a corrupt ceremonial, whose forms had

the young are presented to GOD, after giving forth a confession of their faith. This would not be an unbecoming approval of their Catechism."—*Tracts*, vol. iii., p. 288.

The practice of auricular confession he desired to see reformed and modified, not entirely done away with. "I have often told you," he writes to Farel, "that I should have thought it unwise to abolish confession in our churches, unless the rite which I have lately introduced be established in its place." This custom was that of a personal and private interview of communicants with the pastor, previous to each sacramental occasion. It does not appear that Calvin succeeded in enforcing this duty to any great extent. Indeed, he himself observes in the same connexion: "It is no new thing that pious souls should fear our falling back into superstition, whenever they hear of our establishing anything that has even a *remote similarity* to Popish inventions. Although I cannot expel these doubts from their minds, for we have not the means of doing so, I may express the wish that they may be somewhat careful *to separate the good wheat from the chaff and the tares*."—HENRY's *Life of Calvin*, I., 142.

long enough weighed upon and wearied the souls of men. It went back for authority and inspiration to the law and to the testimony of GOD.

Calvin's form of worship is distinguished by a plain and logical structure. The several acts of devotion follow in progressive series, commencing with those which are more primary and preparative, and culminating in the highest exercises of adoration and faith. This systematic character places it in marked contrast with other formularies, taken from the old mass-books; the proper order and connexion of whose parts it is sometimes difficult for a mind not educated in their use to discover.

In Calvin's service for the morning of the LORD's Day, the reading of a portion of the Holy Scriptures, with the Ten Commandments, is made introductory to the prayers. When this reading, performed by a clerk, is finished, the minister enters the desk, and begins with a sentence of invocation; then calling the people to accompany him in prayer, he proceeds to the confession of sins, and supplication for grace. This ended,*

* Here would naturally come a declaration of forgiveness, such as that in the Anglican ritual; and so Calvin designed: but the prejudices of the times prevented the insertion of this feature.

the congregation unite in praise, singing one of
the Psalms of David.   Then, the minister having
prayed again, invoking the Divine favour, begins
the sermon.   This exercise, being a spiritual
instruction, forms part of the service of Divine
worship, and prepares the way for the prayer
of intercession which follows it, and which is the
longest of these forms; and the whole is terminated,
unless the Communion be administered, with the
LORD's Prayer, the Creed, and the Benediction.

"There is none of us," says he, "but must acknowledge it to be very
useful that, after the general confession, some striking promise of
Scripture should follow, whereby sinners might be raised to the hopes
of pardon and reconciliation. And I would have introduced this
custom from the beginning, but some fearing that the novelty of it
would give offence, I was over easy in yielding to them, so the thing
was omitted, and now it would not be seasonable to make any change;
because the greatest part of our people begin to rise up before we
come to the end of the confession."   Therefore he advises those he
writes to, whilst they had it in their power, to accustom their people
to an absolution, as well as a confession.—*Epist. de Quibusd. Eccles.
Ritib.* p. 206. BINGHAM, *Works*, II. 762. Although omitted, for
the above reasons, in the Genevan Liturgy, this absolution must
have been inserted in Calvin's Liturgy of Strasburg, since it is from
that formulary that the absolution in the Book of Common Prayer
was taken.

To some extent, this usage was introduced into the French churches
upon Calvin's advice; as we learn from a canon passed at the second
General Synod, Paris, 1565: "That such churches as were accustomed upon sacrament days, or other Sabbaths, after the confession of
sins, to pronounce a general absolution, may, if they please, continue
in it: but where this custom is not introduced, the Synod adviseth
the churches not to admit it, because of the dangerous consequences
which may ensue."—QUICK's *Synodicon:* London, 1692: Can. 4.

Respecting the degree of strictness with which these forms of worship should be observed, Calvin's design evidently was, that no deviation be allowed from those parts which are *prescribed*. "As to what concerns a form of prayer and ecclesiastical rites," says he, in a letter to the Protector Somerset, "I highly approve of it that there be a certain form, from which the ministers be not allowed to vary : That first, some provision be made to help the simplicity and unskilfulness of some ; secondly, that the consent and harmony of the churches one with another may appear ; and lastly, that the capricious giddiness and levity of such as affect innovations may be prevented. To which end I have showed that a Catechism will be very useful. Therefore there ought to be a stated Catechism, a stated form of prayer, and adminstration of the sacraments."*

For voluntary and extemporaneous prayer, Calvin made special provision. The prayer before sermon in the service for the LORD's Day, is left to the minister's choice ; and all other services of public prayer, whether on week-days or on the afternoon of the Sabbath, are unrestricted and

* CALVIN, *Epis. ad Protector. Angl.*, p. 41. BINGHAM, II., p. 747.

free. At such times, the preacher is to use "such words in prayer as may seem to him good, suiting his prayer to the occasion, and the matter whereof he treats." Only in those general supplications, which from their nature must be uniform, as they express common wants and desires, the reformer required a close adherence to the public formularies of the Church. This union of free prayer with the rigid use of a Liturgy, was the marked and peculiar excellence of the Genevan worship. Nor was it an impracticable theory, destined to expire with its founder. The experience of three centuries has tested its adequacy and utility. Frequent ecclesiastical enactments secured the observance of this practice in the Reformed Church of France, so long as the synodical government and effective discipline of that Church were suffered to exist. All pastors were required by their ordination vows, to use the liturgical forms in the " public prayers and administration of the sacraments ;" while for all secondary occasions they were left to provide by extempore prayer. The fact that such a combination of free prayer with the use of a liturgy has continued under circumstances most adverse for so long a period, down to the present day,

fully confutes the objection that these methods
are incompatible, and that their connexion must
necessarily result in the relinquishment of the one
or the other. Nor can we fail to perceive in the
successful working of this arrangement, an instance
of the far-reaching penetration of our Reformer;
who thus attained the just and happy medium, as
desirable in our own day as it was then, between
a servile bondage to forms, and a neglect of
the order and symmetry of the service of GOD's
house. His views are therefore correctly rendered
by the excellent Vinet, who says : "There are
good reasons why the minister ought to abstain
from introducing changes of his own into the
worship of GOD, except in cases of real necessity,
such as private or public calamities. The minister is bound to the Liturgy, which belongs not to
him, but is the utterance of the congregation, to
which he does but lend his own individual voice."*

The simplicity upon which this ritual was
framed, pervaded also the manner of its celebration. The churches of Geneva had been stripped
of all their ancient garniture; no symbol of worship remained except the Cross, which for some
years was suffered to stand on the towers of the

* *Théologie Pastorale*, p. 221.

churches.* The altar was replaced by a Communion-table; the baptismal fonts were at first
removed, though afterwards restored;† the prayers
were said, and the Bible read, from the pulpit.
Instead of variegated vestments, the garb of the
ministers was the plain black robe with em-
broidered lappets, the bands, and the black velvet
cap, which were afterwards commonly worn for
many years by the Calvinistic clergy of France,
Holland, and Scotland.‡

* *Régistres du Conseil d'Etat à Genève*, 1556. *Chroniques de
Roset*, in the Library of Geneva, VI. 9. *Le Jubilé de la Réformation* :
Geneva, 1835, p. 93. " On the summit of the tower of St. Peter's
there was yet standing *a large cross* surmounting a gilded ball of
copper, upon which God sent a thunderbolt on the 12th of August
[1556], at about nine o'clock in the forenoon, the lords being seated
at council. The lightning made in the said ball a couple of holes, of
the length of two fingers ; then went down by the stem of the cross
to the belfry, which was roofed with tin, and burned it down to the
clock. Then was it seen that ten brave fellows attacked this fire
with extraordinary hardihood ; for the burning sparks rained down
on their heads, and the height and difficulty of the place must needs
have precipitated them down, if God had not marvellously preserved
them, as He did also the whole city ; for the powder-magazine stood
not five feet beyond the fall of the sparks, which as well with wine
as with water were extinguished, no further damage occurring than
such as was done to the spire upon which stood the cross ; on whose
account, as every one said, God had done this thing, *willing to
purge this church of such relics*."

† HENRY'S *Life of Calvin*, p. 1, c. 9.

‡ This costume, differing considerably from the academic gown now
worn by ministers of the Church of Scotland as well as on the Continent, seems to have become entirely obsolete at the present day.
Calvin, like the ministers of his time, was in the habit of wearing also
a "long gown or robe" in the street ; "for which he never met but

The posture of the people during prayer seems, in the early days of the Reformation, to have been that of kneeling. We infer as much from the remark of Calvin quoted on a preceding page, respecting the introduction of a form of absolution. The fact is indicated also by a canon of the Book of Discipline of the French churches, adopted in 1559, in the following words :

"That great irreverence which is found in divers persons, who at public and private prayers do neither uncover their heads nor bow their knees, shall be reformed; which is a matter repugnant unto piety, and giveth suspicion of pride, and scandalizes them that fear God. Wherefore all pastors shall be advised, as also elders and heads of families, carefully to oversee, that in time of prayer all persons, without exception or acceptation, do evidence by these exterior signs the inward humility of their hearts, and homage which they yield to God ; unless any one be hindered from so doing by sickness or otherwise.*

with one rebuff in all his life, and that from a silly woman who declaimed against long garments," etc. She pretended to prove this from the Gospel, saying, Is it not written, They shall come to you in long garments ? Calvin says, "he left her, in despair of convincing such ignorance."—*Ep. to Farel*, BINGHAM, p. 758.

* *Book of Disc.*, c. 10, art. 1. QUICK's *Synodicon*.

"Calvin himself," says Bingham, "speaking of kneeling at public

While thus providing for the office of prayer, our Reformer introduced also the regular practice of congregational singing. To him we are all indebted for this feature of Divine worship, which was directly copied from the Church of Geneva into the Scottish and Anglican services.* At his suggestion it was that Clement Marot and Theodore Beza translated the Psalms of David into French verse, and set them to simple and appropriate airs. A volume containing some portion of these psalms made its appearance at Geneva, with a preface by Calvin, in 1543; but the collection was not completed before the year 1561.†

In a survey of the Calvinistic worship, this interesting feature of Psalmody must not be omitted. It belongs peculiarly and characteristically to that worship. The Reformers of Swit-

prayer (which is the law of France and Geneva), says, 'If it be asked whether this be an human tradition, which any man may refuse or neglect at pleasure : I answer, It is so human, as also to be divine. It is of God, as it is part of that decency commended to us by the Apostle, 1 Cor. xiv. 40. But it is of men, as it particularly points out and specifies what the Scripture only declares in general.'"— BINGHAM, p. 728.

* In Scotland by John Knox, when he introduced the Genevan Order of Worship. In England the custom of congregational singing of psalms, "as was used among the Protestants of Geneva," was borrowed by the Church of England as early as 1559.—STRYPE, *Life of Archbishop Grindal*, b. i., c. 3.

† SAYOUS, *Etudes Littéraires sur les Ecrivains Français de la Réformation*, I. 26.

zerland and Scotland did not, as we often hear,
deprive their ritual of a responsive and popular
character. They did no more than separate the
functions of minister and people into the distinct
duties of reading and singing. The Psalms are
the responsive part of Calvin's Liturgy. These
choral services embodied the acts of adoration,
praise, and thanksgiving, which are scarcely noticed
in the forms of prayer; while in the latter, the
offices of intercession, supplication, and teaching
were assigned to the minister alone. The prayers,
by constant use made familiar to the people, were
to be followed silently or in subdued tones; the
psalms and hymns constituted their audible utterance in the sacred ministrations.

This portion of Divine service was taken directly
from the Roman Catholic Church, where it had
been preserved from the Jewish and early Christian worship. Nor did our Reformers reject those
other ancient Hymns which for ages had been
closely united with the Psalms in public devotion.
The *Te Deum*, the *Song of Simeon*, the *Magnificat*,
were likewise transferred in a metrical shape to
the Protestant ritual. None of these, perhaps,
has been more frequently and heartily used, in the
solemnities of the Church and in private acts of

praise, than the sublime Hymn of Ambrose and Augustine.

To anticipate the idea that Calvin's Liturgy may have been modelled after or suggested by the English Book of Common Prayer, we have only to note here, besides their general dissimilarity, that the Geneva formulary was published in 1543, (and composed several years earlier,) whereas the First Book of Edward VI. was not issued until 1549. On the other hand, we shall elsewhere see, that what little these forms have in common was borrowed from the Genevan into the Anglican form.

With regard to festivals, Calvin retained, besides the Sabbath, those only that relate to the great periods of our Saviour's life, and that which commemorates the outpouring of the Holy Spirit at Pentecost. Indeed, he would have preferred the retention of those festivals alone which fall upon the LORD's Day: transferring to the Sundays that immediately precede and follow, the celebration of such epochs as were observed on other days. But in this reform, as in some others, his wishes were thwarted by popular prejudices, and by the opposition of his colleagues.

Christmas, Good Friday, Easter, Ascension Day,

and Whitsunday, were the five feasts of the Reformed Church. Of these, Christmas and Easter
are celebrated with peculiar solemnity, as two
out of the four sacramental occasions in the year.
As to the frequency of celebrating the LORD's
Supper, the Reformer's views differed again from
those prevalent at Geneva. He was favourable to
a much more frequent observance than the people
were willing to adopt. "We should have much
wished," he says, " to partake of the LORD's Supper
every month ; but when I found so few that
allowed themselves to be convinced, it seemed
better to spare the weakness of the people's faith,
than to strive obstinately against it. I took care,
however, that it should be remarked in the public
acts, that our custom was defective,* so that those
who come after may have more freedom and ease
in correcting it."†

For the frequency of public services of worship,
Calvin made abundant provision in the churches

---

* "Let the Holy Supper of Our Lord JESUS CHRIST be in as
frequent use as practicable in His Church, according to His own
institution, and as it was observed in the Ancient Church. . . . .
And although, for the present, we are of opinion that it be administered four times a year, it is, nevertheless, a defect that it be celebrated
too seldom."—*Ordonnances Ecclesiastiques*, tit. I., c. 4, art. 149.
Quoted by GAUSSEN, *Sermons*, p. 168.

† *Calvini Epistolæ*, 361. Quoted by HENRY.

of Geneva. Prayers with sermon were said on every day of the week.* On the Sabbath there were three services, one of which was for catechetical instruction. On Monday, Tuesday, and Friday, there was a service at the cathedral, to be attended by all the magistrates of the city. On Thursday took place the weekly expository exercise, called the " *Congregation*," the object of which was " to uphold the purity of the clergy, whether of the city or of the country. At this meeting, every minister was to discourse in his turn on the portion of Scripture appointed for the day. After the sermon, the ministers were to withdraw and make their remarks, especially on the preacher. If any controversy arose on matters of doctrine, they were to employ their best endeavours to preserve union ; and if they failed in this, the elders of the church were to give their opinion on the subject, and strive to restore peace."† This expository service was imitated, as we shall see, in Scotland,

---

* Daily prayers, but without sermon, are still said in the churches of Geneva. See Preface to *La Liturgie de Genève*, 1820. The Thursday service, called "Congregation," is also kept up.

† HENRY's *Life of Calvin*, c. 5. For an interesting specimen of the manner in which these conferences were conducted, see a small tract on the doctrine of Election, entitled, " *Congregation faite en l'Eglise de Genève, par Maître Jean Calvin: à Genève*, 1562 : re-printed 1835."

and thence transferred to the Church of England. Magistrates, soldiers, and people were alike required to attend these week-day services. The students of the academy or university founded by Calvin were to be present at Divine worship every Wednesday in the cathedral, as well as three times on the Sabbath. The city garrison, by a later regulation, were directed to attend prayers twice every day. And here let us observe, in passing, one of those beautiful customs that belong peculiarly to the religious times of which we speak. At every gate of the city, a soldier knelt down and repeated aloud a prayer, before the portal was closed at night, and before it was opened in the morning.* Truly, with such habits of devotion, and such facilities for the spiritual culture of its people, Geneva deserved the eulogy of Knox, when he called it "The most perfect school of CHRIST that ever was on earth."† "GOD hath made of Geneva," says an old writer, "His Bethlehem ; that is to say, His *house of bread.*"‡

This brief analysis of Calvin's order of worship brings us to the examination of the forms of prayer which he composed, as they are contained in the

* HENRY's *Life of Calvin*, p. 2, c. 4.
† M'CRIE's *Life of Knox*, period 5.
‡ *Le Chroniqueur, etc.*, p. 145.

Liturgy of Geneva. That ritual, we have already stated, was published in 1543, though, doubtless, in use among the ministers of Geneva for several years preceding. We find it, as originally drawn up, among the writings of Calvin, both in French and in Latin; nor is it certain which of these languages was the medium of its first publication. With more or less modification, it constitutes the basis of all the Reformed Liturgies, and is now used throughout the churches of Switzerland, France, and the Calvinistic communion in Germany.*

THE FORM OF CHURCH PRAYERS.

On week-days the minister useth such words in prayer as may seem to him good, suiting his prayer to the occasion, and the matter whereof he treats in preaching.

* See the original French in Calvin's *Opuscules*, Geneva, 1566, 1 vol. folio; and the Latin in the Amsterdam edition of 1667. As now used in the Church of Geneva, Calvin's formulary has been altered in some particulars, to suit the prevailing heterodoxy. Compare LA LITURGIE, *Ou la Manière de célébrer le Service Divin dans l'Eglise de Genève:* 1820. We have followed the original in our translation, adding only some rubrical explanations from the modern Liturgy. See HENRY'S *Life of Calvin*, p. 1, c. 7; also *Calvin and the Swiss Reformation*, by JOHN SCOTT, M.A., p. 341; and a *Notice sur la Vie et les Ouvrages de Calvin.* Paris: pp. 15, 43.

In 1545, Calvin prepared for the church at Strasburg, to which he had ministered during his temporary exile from Geneva in 1538—1541, a Liturgy differing but slightly from that of Geneva.

For the Lord's Day in the morning is commonly used the Form ensuing. After the reading of the appointed chapters of Holy Scripture, the Ten Commandments are read. Then the minister begins thus :

INVOCATION.

Our help is in the name of the LORD, who made heaven and earth. Amen.

EXHORTATION.

Brethren, let each of you present himself before the LORD, with confession of his sins and offences, following in heart my words.

CONFESSION. *

Lord GOD! Eternal and Almighty Father: We acknowledge and confess before thy holy majesty, that we are poor sinners; conceived and born in guilt and in corruption, prone to do evil, unable of ourselves to do any good; who, by reason of our depravity, transgress without end thy holy

---

* The origin of this prayer has been a matter of some speculation. Henry, the biographer of Calvin, refers it to the Missal, where, however, we find no trace of such a form. Ebrard (*Reformirtes Kirchenbuch*) ascribes it to Œcolampadius. Current opinion in France has attributed it to Theodore Beza, who used this prayer at the Colloquy of Poissy; but it existed already in the Liturgy of Geneva. We have no reason to doubt Calvin's title to its authorship. The point is one of some interest, as this prayer is to be traced in all the Reformed Liturgies, and even in the Anglican Prayer-book, where it will be found with some alterations.

commandments. Therefore we have drawn upon ourselves, by thy just sentence, condemnation and death. But, O LORD! with heartfelt sorrow we repent and deplore our offences! we condemn ourselves and our evil ways, with true penitence beseeching that thy grace may relieve our distress.

Be pleased then to have compassion upon us, O most gracious GOD! Father of all mercies; for the sake of thy Son JESUS CHRIST our Lord. And in removing our guilt and our pollution, grant us the daily increase of the grace of thine Holy Spirit; that acknowledging from our inmost hearts our own unrighteousness, we may be touched with sorrow that shall work true repentance ; and that thy Spirit, mortifying all sin within us, may produce the fruits of holiness and of righteousness well-pleasing in thy sight : Through JESUS CHRIST our Lord.   Amen.

This done, shall be sung in the congregation a Psalm ; then the minister shall begin afresh to pray, asking of GOD the grace of his Holy Spirit, to the end that his word may be faithfully expounded, to the honour of his name, and to the edification of the church; and that it be received in such humility and obedience as are becoming.

The form thereof is at the discretion of the minister.

[Prayer which the ministers are accustomed to make.*

FOR ILLUMINATION.

Most gracious GOD, our heavenly Father! in whom alone dwelleth all fulness of light and wisdom: Illuminate our minds, we beseech thee, by thine Holy Spirit, in the true understanding of thy word. Give us grace that we may receive it with reverence and humility unfeigned. May it lead us to put our whole trust in thee alone; and so to serve and honour thee, that we may glorify thy holy name, and edify our neighbours by a good example. And since it hath pleased thee to number us among thy people: O help us to pay thee the love and homage that we owe, as children to our Father, and as servants to our Lord. We ask this for the sake of our Master and Saviour, who hath taught us to pray, saying: OUR FATHER, &c. †]

---

* This prayer does not properly belong to the Liturgy, but is that used by Calvin and his colleagues in this part of the service, and is given at the commencement of several of his sermons.

† Here Calvin was accustomed to introduce the Apostles' Creed; which, however, in the Liturgy of Geneva, and in all the formularies framed upon it, occurs at the conclusion of the service. See *Notice sur la Vie de Calvin*, p. 15.

At the end of the sermon, the minister having made exhortation to prayer, beginneth thus:

INTERCESSION.

Almighty GOD, our heavenly Father! who hast promised to grant our requests in the name of thy well-beloved SON: Thou hast taught us in his name also to assemble ourselves together, assured that he shall be present in our midst, to intercede for us with thee, and obtain for us all things that we may agree on earth to ask thee. Wherefore, having met in thy presence, dependent on thy promise, we earnestly beseech thee, O gracious GOD and Father! for his sake who is our only Saviour and Mediator, that of thy boundless mercy thou wilt freely pardon our offences; and so lift up our thoughts and draw forth our desires toward thyself, that we may seek thee according to thy holy and reasonable will.

FOR RULERS.

Heavenly Father! who hast bidden us pray for those in authority over us: We entreat thee to bless all princes and governors, thy servants, to whom thou hast committed the administration of justice; and especially   *   *   *   May it please

thee to grant them the daily increase of thy good
Spirit, that with true faith acknowledging JESUS
CHRIST, thy Son our Saviour, to be King of
kings and Lord of lords, unto whom thou hast
given all power in heaven and on earth : they
may seek to serve thee and exalt thy rule in their
dominions. May they govern their subjects, the
creatures of thy hand and the sheep of thy
pasture, in a manner well-pleasing in thy sight ;
so that as well here as throughout all the earth,
thy people, being kept in peace and quiet, may
serve thee in all godliness and honesty ; and we,
being delivered from the fear of our enemies, may
pass the time of our life in thy praise.

FOR PASTORS.

Almighty Saviour ! we pray for all whom thou
hast appointed pastors of thy believing people,
who are intrusted with the care of souls and the
dispensing of thy holy Gospel. Guide them by
thy Spirit, and make them faithful and loyal
ministers of thy glory. May they ever hold this
end before them : that by them, all poor wandering sheep may be gathered in and made subject to
the LORD JESUS CHRIST, the Shepherd and Bishop
of their souls, and in him daily grow up and

increase in all righteousness and truth. Deliver
thy churches from the mouth of ravenous wolves
and hirelings, who seek only their own ambition
or profit, and not the exaltation of thy holy name,
and the safety of thy flock.

FOR ALL CONDITIONS OF MEN.

Most gracious GOD, Father of all mercies: We
beseech thee for every class and condition of our
fellow-men. Thou who wouldst be acknowledged as
the Saviour of all mankind, in the redemption made
by thy Son JESUS CHRIST: Grant that such as
are yet strangers to thy knowledge, in darkness
and captivity to ignorance and error, may, by the
enlightening of thy Spirit and the preaching of
thy word, be led into the right way of salvation;
which is to know thee, the only true GOD, and JESUS
CHRIST, whom thou hast sent. May those whom
thou hast already visited with thy grace, and
enlightened with the knowledge of thy word, grow
daily in all godliness, and be enriched with thy
spiritual gifts. So that we all, with one heart and
one voice, may ever praise thee, giving honour and
worship to thy CHRIST, our Lord, Lawgiver, and
King.

FOR AFFLICTED PERSONS.

God of all comfort! We commend to thee those whom thou art pleased to visit and chasten with any cross or tribulation; the nations whom thou dost afflict with pestilence, war, or famine; all persons oppressed with poverty, imprisonment, sickness, banishment, or any other distress of body or sorrow of mind: That it may please thee to show them thy fatherly kindness, chastening them for their profit; to the end that in their hearts they may turn unto thee, and being converted, may receive perfect consolation, and deliverance from all their woes.

FOR PERSECUTED CHRISTIANS.

More especially we commend to thee our poor brethren scattered abroad under the tyranny of Antichrist, who are destitute of the pasture of life, and deprived of the privilege of publicly calling on thy holy name. We pray for those who are confined as prisoners, or otherwise persecuted by the enemies of thy Gospel. May it please thee, O Father of mercies! to strengthen them by the virtue of thy Spirit, in such sort that they faint not, but constantly abide in thy holy calling. Succour them, help them as thou knowest they may need; console them in their afflictions; maintain them in thy safe keeping; defend them against the rage of devouring wolves; and augment within them all the graces of thy Spirit, that whether in life or death, they may glorify thy name.

FOR THE CONGREGATION.

Finally, O GOD our Father! Grant also unto us, who are here gathered in the name of thy Holy Child JESUS, to hear his word [and to celebrate his holy Supper], that we may rightly and unfeignedly perceive our lost estate by nature, and the condemnation we have deserved and heaped up to ourselves by disobedient lives. So that conscious that in ourselves there dwelleth no good thing, and that our flesh and blood cannot inherit thy kingdom, with our whole affections we may give ourselves up in firm trust to thy beloved Son, JESUS CHRIST our Lord, our only Saviour and Redeemer. And that he, dwelling in us, may mortify within us the old Adam, renewing us for that better life, wherein we shall exalt and glorify thy blessed and worthy name, ever, world without end.* Amen.

* We have here omitted a long paraphrase of the LORD's Prayer, which in the original is appended to this intercession, but which finds no place in the modern Liturgy of Geneva.

THE LORD'S PRAYER.

Our Father which art in heaven, Hallowed be thy name: Thy kingdom come: Thy will be done in earth as it is in heaven: Give us this day our daily bread: And forgive us our debts, as we forgive our debtors: And lead us not into temptation, but deliver us from evil: For thine is the kingdom, and the power, and the glory, for ever. Amen.

THE CREED.

Lord, increase our faith.

I believe in GOD the Father Almighty, Maker of heaven and earth; and in JESUS CHRIST, his only Son our Lord, who was conceived by the Holy Ghost, born of the Virgin Mary, suffered under Pontius Pilate, was crucified, dead, and buried; He descended into hell; the third day He rose again from the dead; He ascended into heaven, and sitteth on the right hand of GOD the Father Almighty; from thence He shall come to judge the quick and the dead. I believe in the HOLY GHOST; the Holy Catholic Church; the communion of saints; the forgiveness of sins; the resurrection of the body, and the life everlasting. Amen.

THE BLESSING.

Which is pronounced at the departure of the people, according as our Lord hath commanded in the Law,—Numb. vi. 23.

The Lord bless thee, and keep thee;

The Lord make his face shine upon thee, an be gracious unto thee;

The Lord lift up his countenance upon thee, and give thee peace.

Whereunto is added, to remind the people of the duty of alms-giving, as it is customary upon leaving the church,

Depart in peace. Remember the poor; and the GOD of peace be with you. Amen.

II.

Calvin's Last Communion.

"As in heathen rites all was external, there the display of imagery
abounded. But the sanctuary of Christianity is in the heart; hence
the poetry it inspires must always flow from tenderness of feeling.
It is not the splendours of the Christian heaven that we can oppose
to the pagan Olympus; but those phases of *sorrow and innocence,
old age and death,* which assume an air of serene elevation and repose,
under the shelter of religious hopes, whose wings are spread out to
cover the miseries of life. It seems to me untrue, then, that the
Protestant religion is devoid of poetry, though its customs of worship
have less that is brilliant than those of the Catholic faith."

MAD. DE STAEL, *de l'Allemagne,* p. iv. c. 4.

IT was Easter Sunday at Geneva, in the year
1564. The doors of St. Peter's Cathedral were
thrown open, and multitudes pressing eagerly
through them, soon filled the broad area within.
A festival of no little interest and importance
convoked these crowds: for on Easter the Church
of Geneva was accustomed to celebrate, with
more solemnity than at other periods of the year,
the ordinance of the LORD's Supper. Looking
down the long Gothic nave to the opposite end
of the building, one might discover by the dim
light of the stained windows, the Holy Table
made ready with its pure covering, and the

sacred vessels glistening upon it. On each side were seated the ministers of the church, and behind them the grave syndics and other magistrates of the city, in their velvet robes of office. But it was not to these august preparatives that the eyes of the citizens were directed. Those who had obtained room within, and the many who lingered around the entrance, seemed alike in expectancy of some arrival which was the object of this unusual curiosity. It is Calvin who is coming; Calvin, whose voice has sounded so often along those arches, but who never again will stand in yonder pulpit to address his people. He comes in his last sickness to participate once more with his beloved flock in the emblems of the Redeemer's love. There is a deep silence of sorrow pervading this vast assembly, broken only by here and there a sob of grief not to be repressed. But now the throng parts, and through its midst is carried on a chair the feeble and emaciated frame of the great Reformer. He is not old, but toil of mind has outworn the body. The pallid, sunken cheeks show the ravages of disease; yet the large eyes are lustrous still, and they glance with more than common earnestness over the sea of faces that are turned to meet them.

Now the chair is lowered to its place before the
Communion-table; and the breathless silence is
broken by a voice from the pulpit at one side of
the church, commencing the usual service of the
Sabbath worship.   With what meaning fall upon
the hearing of the multitude those prayers which
are so familiar to their ears, as uttered by one
who shall speak them no more on earth!   The
introductory service is over, and the sermon com-
mences.   Beza is the preacher: Beza, long the
most faithful disciple, the most able successor of
the great Reformer; he who in a few days will
have occasion to utter those words of heart-broken
affection: " Now that Calvin is dead, life will be
less sweet, and death less bitter."*   We need not
be told that deep feeling showed itself in his discourse; that more than once his voice trembled,
or was choked with a deep emotion.

The sermon over, the preacher descends from
the pulpit, and going to the sacred table, reads
the exhortation preparatory to the ordinance.
The consecrating prayer is said, and Beza carries
to his illustrious master the symbols of redemption.   Then the vast congregation, coming forward
by groups, receive the blessed elements in silent

* GILLIES' *Historical Collections*, book ii. ch. 2.

devotion; and when all is through, they join in
the concluding hymn of praise. Calvin is not
mute; his tremulous voice rises with the rest,
and " on his dying countenance," says Beza,
whose eyes are fixed upon his master, " was not
obscurely indicated a holy joy."* They sang, as
usual, the Song of Simeon, with which, in the
Calvinistic worship, the celebration of the Supper
is always closed.†

> Now let thy servant, LORD!
>   At length depart in peace;
> According to thy word,
>   My waiting soul release:
> For thou my longing eyes hast spared
> To see thy saving grace declared.
>
> To see thy saving grace,
>   That soon dispensed abroad,
> The nations shall embrace,
>   And find their help in GOD:
> A light to lighten every land,
> The glory of thy chosen band.

* BEZA's *Life of Calvin*, prefixed to Calvin's Tracts, vol. i.
† The words and melody of this hymn are still in use; the former
composed by Clement Marot, 1543; the latter attributed to Guillaume
Franc, 1552. We subjoin the original words:

> Laisse-moi désormais,   Salut qu'en l'univers
> Seigneur, aller en paix,   Tant de peuples divers,
> Car selon ta promesse,   Vont reçevoir et croire;
> Tu fais voir à mes yeux   Ressource des petits,
> Le salut glorieux   Lumière des Gentils,
> Que j'attendais sans cesse.   Et d'Israël la gloire.

—*Les Pseaumes de David, mis en Vers François,* par CLEMENT
MAROT et TH. DE BEZE.

Thus consecrated by his own dying participation, Calvin's form for the celebration of the LORD's Supper* has come down to us; and we present it here as a precious legacy of that illustrious mind.

THE MANNER OF CELEBRATING THE LORD'S SUPPER.

Note, that on the Sabbath before the Supper is to be celebrated, it must be announced to the people, in order that each may prepare and dispose himself worthily to receive it.†   Also, that children be not brought to the Communion, until they have been well instructed, and have made profession of their faith, in the Church.   And again, that strangers, who are yet rude and ignorant, may come to be taught in private.

On the day of the celebration, the minister in the conclusion of his sermon adverts to it, or else, if the matter be in hand, refers his whole discourse to the same, expounding to the people what our

---

* *Opuscules de* J. CALVIN. We have introduced from the Liturgy now used at Geneva some of the rubrical directions which serve to indicate the manner in which these forms are used.

† Calvin recommended that persons intending to approach the LORD's Table should call upon their pastor previous to the celebration of the sacrament, for the purpose of receiving spiritual instruction and counsel. A similar custom was enjoined by the Church of Scotland: — "That every master and mistress of household come themselves and their family, so many as be come to maturity, before the Minister and the Elders, and give confession of their faith," — *First Book of Discipline,* ch. xi.

E

LORD *would say and signify by this mystery, and after what manner he would have us receive it.*

The following prayer is to be added to the usual prayer after the sermon:

THE INVOCATION.*

Most gracious GOD! we beseech thee, that as thy Son hath not only once offered up his body and blood upon the cross for the remission of our sins, but hath also vouchsafed them unto us, for our meat and drink unto life eternal: So thou wilt grant us grace, with sincere hearts and fervent desires, to accept this great blessing at his hands. May we by lively faith partake of his body and blood, yea, of himself, true GOD and man, the only bread from heaven, which giveth life unto our souls. Suffer us no longer to live unto ourselves, according to a corrupt and sinful nature; but may He live in us, and lead us to the life that is holy, blessed, and unchangeable for

---

* We shall not specify the many points of resemblance which this service bears with the beautiful form of administering this ordinance in the Reformed Dutch Liturgy. It will be easy for the reader to compare them. Nor need we add that we have here the original, of which the Dutch form is an arrangement, and in some respects an improvement. That service, however, has not been improved by transferring the prayer of Invocation from its place as here given, to the close of the Exhortation.

ever. Thus make us true partakers of the new and everlasting testament, which is the covenant of grace. And thus assure us of thy willingness ever to be our gracious Father; not imputing unto us our sins, but that we may magnify thy name by our words and works, providing us as thy beloved children and heirs with all things necessary for our good. Fit us, O heavenly FATHER! so to celebrate at this time the blessed remembrance of thy beloved Son. Enable us profitably to contemplate his love, and show forth the benefits of his death: That receiving fresh increase of strength in thy faith and in all good works, we may with greater confidence call thee our FATHER, and evermore rejoice in thee: Through JESUS CHRIST, our Redeemer. Amen.

THE CREED.

Let us now make profession of our faith in the doctrine of the Christian Religion, wherein we all purpose by GOD's grace to live and to die.

I believe in GOD the Father Almighty, Maker of heaven and earth: and in JESUS CHRIST, his only Son our Lord, who was conceived by the Holy Ghost, born of the Virgin Mary, suffered under Pontius Pilate, was crucified, dead and

buried; He descended into hell; the third day He
rose again from the dead, He ascended into heaven,
and sitteth on the right hand of GOD the Father
Almighty; from thence He shall come to judge
the quick and the dead. I believe in the HOLY
GHOST; the holy Catholic Church; the communion of Saints; the forgiveness of sins; the resurrection of the body, and the life everlasting.
Amen.

Then the minister maketh this

EXHORTATION.

Attend to the words of the institution of the
holy Supper of our Lord JESUS CHRIST, as they
are delivered by the Apostle Paul.*

For I have received of the LORD that which
also I delivered unto you: That the Lord JESUS,
the same night in which he was betrayed, took
bread; and when he had given thanks, he brake
it, and said, Take, eat; this is my body, which is
broken for you: this do in remembrance of me.
After the same manner also he took the cup, when
he had supped, saying: This cup is the new
testament in my blood: this do ye, as oft as ye

* 1 Cor. xi. 23—30.

drink it, in remembrance of me. For as often as ye eat this bread, and drink this cup, ye do show the LORD's death till he come. Wherefore, whosoever shall eat this bread, and drink this cup of the LORD, unworthily, shall be guilty of the body and blood of the LORD. But let a man examine himself, and so let him eat of that bread, and drink of that cup. For he that eateth and drinketh unworthily, eateth and drinketh damnation to himself, not discerning the LORD's body.

We have heard, brethren, in what manner our LORD celebrated the Supper among his disciples; whence we see that strangers, who are not of the company of the faithful, may not approach it. Wherefore, in obedience to this rule, and in the name and by the authority of our Lord JESUS CHRIST, I excommunicate all idolaters, blasphemers, despisers of GOD, heretics, and all who form sects apart, to break the unity of the Church; all perjurers, all who are rebellious against fathers and mothers, and other superiors, all who are seditious, contentious, quarrelsome, injurious, adulterers, fornicators, thieves, misers, ravishers, drunkards, gluttons, and all others who lead scandalous lives; warning them that they abstain from this Table, lest they pollute and contaminate the sacred food which our Lord JESUS CHRIST giveth only to his faithful servants.

Therefore, according to the exhortation of St. Paul, let each of you examine and prove his own conscience, to know whether he have true repentance of his sins, and sorrow for them; desiring henceforth to lead a holy and godly life; above all, whether he putteth his whole trust in GOD's mercy, and seeketh his whole salvation in JESUS CHRIST; and renouncing all enmity and malice, doth truly and honestly purpose to live in harmony and brotherly love with his neighbour.

If we have this testimony in our hearts before GOD, we may not doubt that he adopteth us for his children, and that our Lord JESUS addresseth his word to us, admitting us to his Table, and presenting us with this holy sacrament, which he bestows upon his followers.

And notwithstanding that we feel many infirmities and miseries in ourselves, as, namely, that we have not perfect faith, and that we have not given ourselves to serve GOD with such zeal as we are bound to do, but have daily to battle with the lusts of our flesh; yet, since the LORD hath graciously been pleased to print his Gospel upon our hearts, in order that we may withstand all unbelief; and hath given us this earnest desire to renounce our own thoughts and follow his righteousness and his holy commandments : therefore we rest assured, that our remaining sins and imperfections do not prevent us from being received of GOD and made worthy partakers of this spiritual food. For we come not to this Supper to testify hereby that we are perfect and righteous in ourselves; but on the contrary, seeking our life in JESUS CHRIST, we acknowledge that we lie in the midst of death.   Let us then look upon this sacrament as a medicine for those who are spiritually sick; and consider that all the worthiness our LORD requireth of us, is that we truly know ourselves, be sorry for our sins, and find our pleasure, joy, and satisfaction in him above.

First, then, we must believe these promises, which JESUS CHRIST, who is infallible truth, hath pronounced with his own lips: That he is truly willing to make us partakers of his body and of his blood, in order that we may wholly possess him, and that he may live in us, and we in him. And although we see here only the Bread and Wine, let us not doubt that he will accomplish spiritually in our souls all that he outwardly exhibits by these visible signs; he will show himself

to be the heavenly bread, to feed and nourish us
unto life eternal. Let us not be unthankful to
the infinite goodness of our LORD, who displays
all his riches and his wealth at this Table, to
distribute them among us. For in giving himself,
he testifies that all he hath is ours. Let us
receive this sacrament as a pledge that the virtue
of his death and passion is imputed unto us for
righteousness; even as though we had suffered in
our own persons. Let none perversely draw back,
when JESUS CHRIST doth gently invite him by
his word. But considering the dignity of his
precious gift, let us present ourselves to him with
ardent zeal, that he may make us capable of receiving it.

And now, to this end, lift up your minds and
hearts on high, where JESUS CHRIST abideth in
the glory of his Father, whence we expect his
coming at our redemption. Dwell not upon these
earthly and corruptible elements, which we see
present to our eyes, and feel with our hands, to
seek him in them, as if he were inclosed in the
Bread or in the Wine. For then only shall our
souls be disposed to receive food and life from his
substance, when they shall thus be lifted up above
worldly things, even unto heaven, and enter into

the kingdom of GOD, where he dwelleth. Let us be satisfied to have this Bread and this Wine for witnesses and signs; seeking spiritually the truth where GOD's word hath promised that we shall find it. *

This done, the ministers distribute the Bread and the Cup to the people, having warned them to come forward with reverence and order. Meanwhile a Psalm is sung, or a portion of the Scripture read, suitable to what is signified by the Sacrament. The Supper being over, is used this or the like

* Here the Liturgy of Geneva as it now stands supplies the omission of the words of the Institution as follows:

The Minister having come down from the pulpit, goeth to the Table, breaketh the Bread, and saith, giving it unto the minister who assists in the distribution:

The Bread which we break, is the communion of the body of JESUS CHRIST our Lord.

Or other words to the like effect. Then he himself partaketh. The other minister, giving him the cup, saith:

The cup of blessing which we bless, is the communion of the blood of JESUS CHRIST our Lord.

Or other words to the like effect. Then he himself partaketh. The same is done at the second Table, where likewise two ministers officiate.

The ministers having communicated, the magistrates, and then all those of the congregation, approach the Table in turn and with order. The men and the women go separately. One of the ministers distributeth the Bread, and the other the Cup, saying to each communicant some words proper to excite devotion. Meanwhile the Reader readeth certain chapters of Holy Scripture suitable to the occasion, and giveth out Psalms or Hymns to be sung.

THANKSGIVING.

Heavenly Father! we give thee immortal praise
and thanks, that upon us poor sinners thou hast
conferred so great a benefit, as to bring us into
the communion of thy Son JESUS CHRIST our
Lord; whom having delivered up to death for us,
thou hast given for our food and nourishment
unto eternal life.   Now, also, grant us grace, that
we may never be unmindful of these things; but
rather carrying them about engraven upon our
hearts, may advance and grow in that faith which
is effectual unto every good work.   Thus, may
the rest of our lives be ordered and followed out
to thy glory and the edification of our neighbours :
Through JESUS CHRIST our Lord ; Who with thee,
O FATHER! and the HOLY GHOST, liveth and
reigneth in the unity of the Godhead, world without end.   Amen.

*Then, all the congregation standing, is sung the
Hymn of Simeon, after which the minister dis-
misses the people with*

THE BLESSING.

The grace of the Lord JESUS CHRIST, and the
love of GOD, and the communion of the HOLY
GHOST, be with you all.   Amen.

III.

Calvin's Daily Offices.

"Prayer to GOD is the chief part, yea, the main thing in religion. For the design of the whole truth respecting salvation, is to teach us that our life depends on GOD, and that whatever belongs to eternal life must be hoped for and expected from him."—CALVIN, *Minor Proph.*, v. 227.

IT is a custom in the Romish Church on a certain feast-day in the year, to take the candles which have been blessed at the altar, and distribute them among the people. These sacred tapers are carried home, and kept with superstitious care, as precious safeguards against all evil. Something better than this has Protestantism done for her worshipping multitudes. The flame that was dimly burning in the damp air of churches, she has kindled in their houses, to be brightly nourished at the family altar. In place of daily masses, of matins, vespers, and nocturns, she has given us the beautiful office of morning and evening prayer in the family and the home. For the gloom of the Gothic chancel, the inarticulate mutter of the priest, and the heedless response of the choir-boy, she has conferred the cheer of the fireside devotion, and the parent's intercessory voice, accompanied by intelligent thought, and awakening pious emotion.

It is a fact truly of no little interest, that wherever the principles of the Reformation have prevailed, they have revived the ancient custom of family worship. The Reformers, while they did not omit provision for the frequent assembling of believers in the sanctuary, yet were evidently most anxious to secure a regular and devout observance of this primal and all-essential duty. Thus one of the very earliest enactments of the Church of Scotland, after recommending daily services of prayer and preaching in the churches, directs that " in private houses the most grave and discreet person use the Common Prayers at morn and night, for the comfort and instruction of others."*

And the Church of France, a few years later, to insure the general observance of this duty, went even so far as to discourage the practice, then incipient, of having daily prayer in the churches, lest it should interfere with the more essential matter of domestic worship. " Churches which, besides their ordinary sermons, are accustomed to morning and evening Common Prayers, on such

* *First Book of Discipline*, ch. xi.

days when there is no preaching, or once a day towards night, when there has been a sermon, are intreated to conform themselves unto those churches which have no such custom; that so superstition, which is likely to follow thereupon, may be prevented, and that visible neglect and contempt of sermons may be avoided; and Family Prayers, which every householder is bound to perform, may be no more neglected."*

In further provision for this important service, the Reformers have furnished us with several forms of family worship; the most remarkable of which are those composed by Calvin, and copied with more or less alteration into all the Reformed rituals. They are familiar to many in this country [America] in a modified shape, as contained in the Liturgy of the Dutch Reformed Church, under the title of "The Morning and Evening Prayers."†

To the second of these prayers, that for the evening, we would call more particular attention. As well for the happiness of the language as for the beauty of the leading thoughts, in which the

* 2nd Synod of Paris, 1565.

† Liturgy of the Reformed Dutch Church. Compare "Several Godly Prayers" of CALVIN, Tracts, vol. ii.; "Private Prayers" in the Palatine Catechism, and in Knox's Liturgy; "Christian Prayers and Meditations," in a volume of Prayers issued by the Parker Society.

suggestions of night and darkness are treated with exquisite feeling, we have long considered this prayer the finest composition of the kind that has fallen under our notice.

THE MORNING PRAYER.

Cause me to hear thy loving-kindness in the morning ; for in thee do I trust.

Cause me to know the way wherein I should walk ; for I lift up my soul unto thee.

Almighty GOD, our Father and Preserver! we give thee thanks that of thy goodness thou hast watched over us the past night, and brought us to this day. We beseech thee, strengthen and guard us by thy Spirit, that we may spend it wholly in thy service, aiming at thy glory, and the salvation of our fellow-men. And even as thou sheddest now the beams of the Sun upon the earth to give light unto our bodies, so illuminate our souls with the brightness of thy Spirit, to guide us in the paths of thine obedience. May all our purpose be this day to honour and serve thee ; may we look for all prosperity to thy blessing only, and seek no object but such as may be pleasing in thy sight. Enable us, O LORD! while we labour for the body, and the life that now is, ever to look beyond unto that heavenly life which thou hast promised thy children. Defend us in soul and body from all harm. Guard us against all assaults of the devil, and deliver us from any dangers that may beset us. And seeing it is a small thing to have begun well, except we also persevere, take us, O LORD! into thy good keeping this day, and all our days; continue and increase thy grace within us, until we shall be perfectly united in the glory of thy Son JESUS CHRIST our Lord, the Sun of Righteousness, who shall replenish our souls with his eternal light and gladness. And that we may obtain all these blessings, be pleased to cast out of thy remembrance all our past offences, and of thy boundless mercy forgive them; as thou hast promised those who call upon thee in sincerity and truth. Hear us, O GOD, our Father and Redeemer! through JESUS CHRIST our Lord: In whose name we pray, as he hath taught us, saying—OUR FATHER, etc.

THE EVENING PRAYER.

Consider and hear me, O Lord; lighten mine eyes, lest I sleep the sleep of death.

I will both lay me down in peace and sleep; for thou, Lord, only makest me to dwell in safety.

O merciful GOD! Eternal light, shining in darkness, thou who dispellest the night of sin, and all blindness of heart: since thou hast appointed the night for rest, and the day for labour; we beseech thee, grant that our bodies may rest in peace and quietness, that afterward they may be able to endure the labour they must bear. Temper our sleep, that it be not disorderly, that we may remain spotless both in body and soul; yea, that our sleep itself may be to thy glory. Enlighten the eyes of our understanding, that we may not sleep in death; but always look for deliverance from this misery. Defend us against all assaults of the devil, and take us into thine holy protection. And although we have not passed this day without greatly sinning against thee, we beseech thee to hide our sins with thy mercy, as thou hidest all things on earth with the darkness of the night, that we may not be cast out from thy presence. Relieve and comfort all those who are afflicted or distressed, in mind, body, or estate: Through JESUS CHRIST our Lord; who hath taught us to pray—OUR FATHER, etc.

The interest with which we regard these beautiful forms is increased by an historical fact con-

nected with one of them. It was in the language
of this "Evening Prayer" that our illustrious
Reformer, John Knox, breathed his dying thoughts
to heaven. Let us hear the account given by his
biographer : "At ten o'clock, they read the Evening Prayer, which they had delayed beyond the
usual hour, from an apprehension that he was
asleep. After this exercise was concluded, Dr.
Preston asked him if he had heard the prayers.
'Would to God,' said he, 'that you and all men
had heard them as I have heard them; I praise
GOD for that heavenly sound.' The doctor rose
up, and Kinyeancleugh sat down before his bed.
About eleven o'clock, he gave a deep sigh, and
said, 'Now it is come.' Bannatyne immediately
drew near, and desired him to think upon those
comfortable promises of our Saviour JESUS CHRIST,
which he had so often declared to others ; and,
perceiving that he was speechless, requested him
to give them a sign that he heard them, and died
in peace. Upon this he lifted up one of his hands,
and sighing twice, expired without a struggle."*

The forms of prayer used by Calvin in the daily
services of the church at Geneva, were not incorporated with his Liturgy; but they have been

* M'CRIE'S *Life*, p. 339.

handed down to us in connexion with some of his discourses. We translate the following service from the preface to Calvin's Lectures on Job. To this service the great Reformer was accustomed to adhere with considerable closeness; except in those petitions that immediately followed the sermon, which always varied with the matter of the discourse. Of these we give a specimen under the head of the "Special Prayer." Each of the published Lectures of Calvin closes with one of these beautiful collects; of which some further examples will be found in another place.

THE DAILY PRAYERS.

INVOCATION.

Our help is in the name of the LORD, who made heaven and earth. Amen.

SUPPLICATION.

Almighty GOD, our Heavenly Father! we invoke thy name, beseeching that it may please thee to turn away thy face from our great and manifold sins and transgressions, by which we have not ceased to draw thine anger upon us. And because we are most unworthy to appear before thy sovereign majesty, be pleased to regard us in thy well-

beloved Son Jesus Christ, and accept the merit
of his death in satisfaction for all our offences;
that by his atonement we may become well-
pleasing in thy sight. Pour down thine Holy
Spirit upon us, illuminating our minds in the true
understanding of thy word. And bestow upon us
grace, that receiving thy truth into our hearts
with humility and fear, we may be led to place all
our trust in thee only, living in thy service and
worship, to the glory of thy holy name. And
since it hath pleased thee to number us among thy
people : O help us to render the love and homage
that we owe thee, as children to our Father, and
as servants to our Lord. We ask this in the
words our blessed Master taught us, saying—Our
Father, etc.

After the Sermon the following Prayers are said:

THE SPECIAL PRAYER.

Almighty God! who hast made known to us in
thy Son the fulness of all blessing and glory : O
grant that we may continue settled and grounded
in Him, nor ever fluctuate from our attachment,
but be so satisfied with his kingship and priesthood, as to deliver ourselves up wholly to his care

and protection. Suffer us not to doubt that by
his grace we shall be sanctified and made acceptable to thee; but relying on him as our Mediator,
may we offer ourselves a sacrifice to him with full
confidence of heart; so striving to glorify thee
through the whole course of our life, that we may
at length be made partakers of that celestial
glory obtained for us by the blood of thine only
begotten Son.

THE GENERAL PRAYER.

Neither ask we these benefits for ourselves only,
but for all people and nations of the earth. Bring
back, O LORD! into the right way of salvation,
all poor captives of ignorance and false doctrine.
Raise up true and faithful ministers of the word,
who shall seek not their own ease and ambition,
but the exaltation of thy Name and the safety of
thy flock. Remove and destroy all sects, heresies,
and errors, which are the nurseries of strife and
dissension in the Church; that all thy people may
be of one heart, and live in brotherly union. Rule
thou and govern with thy Spirit all kings, princes,
and lords, who hold the administration of the
sword; that their dominion be exercised not in
avarice, cruelty, and oppression, or any other evil

and inordinate affection, but in all justice and rectitude. May we also, living under them, pay them due honour and reverence, and lead quiet and peaceable lives, in all godliness and honesty. Be pleased to comfort all distressed and afflicted persons, whom thou dost visit with any kind of cross or tribulation : the nations whom thou chasteneth with war, pestilence, famine, or any other plague; and all men whom thou afflictest with poverty, imprisonment, sickness, banishment, or any other distress of body or affliction of mind. Give them firm patience under their trials, and speedily bring them out of their afflictions. Strengthen and confirm all thy faithful children, who in various places are scattered in Babylonish captivity, under the tyranny of Antichrist; suffering persecution for the testimony of thy heavenly truth. Give them steadfast constancy; console them, nor suffer the rage of rapacious wolves to prevail against them; but enable them to glorify thy name, as well in life as in death. Confirm and defend all thy churches who at this day are labouring and fighting for the holy testimony of thy name. Defeat and overturn all the counsels of their enemies, their machinations and undertakings. So that thy glory may be

revealed, and the kingdom of our Lord JESUS
CHRIST more and more increased and promoted.
These things we ask of thee, as our sovereign
Lord and Master JESUS CHRIST hath taught us to
pray, saying—OUR FATHER, etc.

THE CREED.

ALMIGHTY GOD! we beseech thee, grant us true
perseverance in thy holy faith, and increase it
ever within us: Whereof we make confession,
saying—I BELIEVE, etc.

THE BLESSING

*with which it is customary to dismiss the congre-
gation.*

The grace of GOD the Father, and the peace of
our Lord JESUS CHRIST, by the communication
of the HOLY GHOST, dwell with you evermore.
Amen.

IV.

The Genevan Liturgy in France.

"The French Liturgy is so often mentioned in many parts of their Book of Discipline and Canons, that I think it useless to offer any farther proofs that they have an established Liturgy among them."

BINGHAM.

THE forms of worship we have now presented to view, if interesting for their age and authorship, receive additional lustre from an eventful history. So far as the Churches of France are concerned, that history abounds with passages of a striking character. While in Scotland the Liturgy of John Knox, after a century's existence, became displaced and fell into oblivion; in France the Prayers of Calvin have continued to be generally used, until incorporated with the religion and endeared to the heart of every worshipper. At this day, from every pulpit those beautiful forms of sound words are to be heard as in the first years of the Reformation; and the simple, yet impressive rites of a pure worship, are observed as at the beginning, without servility, but with voluntary faithfulness. It is not alone the intrinsic merit of these prayers that commends them

to so much veneration. Interwoven with them
are associations of the most affecting nature.
Reminiscences of humble meetings of the Reformers, secret convocations in the Desert, occasional seasons of prosperity, and long intervals of
persecution, are entwined about them. These
services of worship, together with the Psalms
dating from the same period, have come down to
us through long ages of dark and bitter trial;
during which, always prized and employed, they
have cheered the faith and fanned the devotion
of thousands. This fact, in the eyes of a French
Protestant, surrounds them with a sanctity and
beauty such as our neglected Scottish Liturgy can
never possess to us. The dearest though saddest
memories of a Martyr-Church are connected with
the modes of worship under which, "in all time
of her tribulation, in all time of her prosperity,"
she has sought and found succour from Heaven.

We shall briefly review the extent of the adoption and retention of these forms in France, within
the past three centuries. The indications of their
prevalence can be gathered only from isolated
allusions through the course of history, in the
total absence of any connected series of statements.

When Calvin communicated to the Churches of France that Confession of Faith which they adopted and retained ever after as their doctrinal basis,* he gave them also the ritual of their worship. The first disseminators of evangelical truth, the colporteurs and peddlers who carried their burdens of religious books from Geneva into all parts of France, acquainted the new converts with these services.† We find them used at the earliest meetings of the Reformed congregations after their ecclesiastical organization in 1555.

The edict issued by Charles IX., in July, 1561, granted them some degree of liberty in the celebration of religious rites. Let us hear these services described by an old Catholic chronicler, who is at no pains to conceal his ill-will for the new sect. "Though all religious assemblies were expressly forbid by the Edict," says Castelnau, "yet they could not refrain from meeting in private houses, where they baptized, married, received the sacraments, and performed all other religious offices after the Geneva Form. In a little time after, their assemblies became so numerous, that the houses in which they usually met were not

* De Felice, *History of the Protestants of France*, p. 89.
† *Ibid.*, p. 73.

sufficient to contain them. However, very few of their chief preachers appeared, and these meetings were for the most part made up of poor ignorant people, who had no other knowledge or doctrines but only the Catechisms and Prayers that were printed in Geneva."*

Among the earliest enactments of the Synods of the French Churches, we find reference to this Liturgy, which, from the outset, had been adopted as their uniform mode of worship. The enforcement of a strict and undeviating adherence to it seem to have constituted one of the chief anxieties of these ecclesiastical bodies, so long as they were permitted to meet and to legislate for the government of the Church. Thus the thirty-first canon of the Discipline established by the first National Synod, which met at Paris, in 1559, declares: " If one or more of the people stir up contention, and do thereby break the Churches' union in any point of Doctrine, or of Discipline, or about the Form of Catechizing, or *Administration of the Sacraments*, or of *Publick Prayers*, or the *Celebration of Marriage*," etc., they shall be exhorted,

* "*Memoirs of the Reigns of Francis II. and Charles IX., of France, by* MICHAEL CASTELNAU, *who was Ambassador for Ten Years at the Court of Queen Elizabeth. Done into English by a Gentleman, and published for his Benefit.*" London, 1734, p. 115.

censured, or excommunicated, according as the case may be. The same penalties are imposed by the thirty-second canon upon any *Minister* stirring up contention about " The Form of our Common Prayers," etc.*

The Eleventh Synod, which met in 1581, ordered that printers publishing the Psalm-book of the Church should not separate from it the Prayers and Catechism, but bind together. An earlier law provides that all persons should bring their Psalm-books with them to Divine service, and reproves those who fail in doing so.†

The Thirteenth Synod, at Montauban in 1594, enacted that " There shall be *no alteration* made in the Forms of Public Prayers and Administration of the Sacraments; the whole having been prudently and piously ordained, and for the most part in plain and express terms of Holy Scripture."‡

At the Fifteenth Synod, Montpellier, 1598,

---

* QUICK's *Synodicon in Gallia Reformata:* a remarkable work well known to bibliophiles, published at London in 1692, by a nonconformist minister, who had collected in these two folio volumes all the acts and decrees of the National Synods of France *from the original registers*, which we believe have never been published in the French.

† *Ibid.*, ch. iii., art. 40.

‡ *Ibid.*, ch. iv., art. 19.

letters were received from Geneva, urging that no innovation be permitted in the Liturgy, singing of Psalms, and Form of Catechizing; which was accordingly ordered.*

By the Synod of St. Maixant, 1609, "All pastors were enjoined to abstain from any new or private methods of their own [in the service of the LORD's Supper], as of reading the words of institution between the ordinary long prayer, and that appointed particularly for this sacrament, etc. Classes and Synods shall have their eyes over those who act contrary to this order, and reduce them to their duty by all befitting censures."†

The Synod which met at Tonneins in 1614, declared that "Even National Synods should not innovate anything in the Confession of Faith, Catechism, Liturgy, and Discipline of the Church; unless the matter had been first proposed by one or more Provinces; and also, unless it were a thing of very great importance."‡

Finally, the Synod of Loudun, the last National Assembly of the French Churches, which met in 1659, after which period the Presbyterian organization of the churches in France was destroyed

* QUICK's *Synodicon*, ch. v., art. 3.   † *Ibid.*, ch. vi., art. 14.
‡ *Ibid.*, ch. viii., art. 8.

by a persecuting government, passed an order for the obtaining of *more accurate editions* of the Liturgy, Catechism, Bible, and Psalms.*

Such value did the suffering Churches of the Reformation in France attach to their venerable Liturgy, and such care did they exhibit in preserving it intact from accidental and designed alteration, that they might hand it down to posterity as they themselves had received it.

Of the Calvinistic forms thus early and extensively brought into use among the French Churches, there are some which have had a distinct and peculiar importance. That beautiful Confession of Sins, which in Calvin's Liturgy introduces the worship for the LORD's Day, is associated with one of the most impressive passages of ecclesiastical history. It was at the famous Colloquy or Conference of Poissy, on the 9th September, 1561, when, by request of Charles IX. and his mother Catherine de Medici, the leaders of Protestantism consented to appear in public debate with the prelates and doctors of Rome, and vindicate the principles of the Reformation. The occasion was brilliant and august. Already the assembly had been convoked in the great

* QUICK's *Synodicon*, etc.

refectory of the convent of Poissy, when the Reformers entered. The young king and his mother
were presiding, attended by a multitude of princes,
courtiers, cardinals, bishops, and theologians; all
arrayed in gorgeous habiliments, and presenting
a spectacle of the most imposing character. At
length the twelve pastors and twenty-two dele-
gates who had been chosen to represent the Reformed faith under these trying circumstances,
were permitted to present themselves before this
assemblage. At their head was Theodore Beza,
whom Calvin had persuaded to assume this re-
sponsible post.* As the deputation advanced up
the aisle, their grave and simple costume forming
a strange contrast with the insignia of prelates
and nobles,† they found themselves separated
from the courtly gathering by a barrier erected
across their way, behind which they were to stand
like criminals at the bar. Nothing troubled by
this indignity, but rather encouraged to look
above all human displays to the Divine tribunal
at which they stood, Beza in the name of his
colleagues turned to the king with a respectful
salutation, and said: " Sire, the help of GOD is
essential to success in whatever undertaking."

* HENRY'S *Calvin*, Part ii., ch. xii.   † DE FELICE, p. 138.

Then immediately kneeling down with them at the barrier, he uttered with fervour the prayer to which we have alluded, beginning with these words : " O Lord God! Father Almighty and Eternal : we acknowledge and confess before thy holy Majesty, that we are miserable sinners."* This ended, he rose, and pronounced his famous defence of the Reformed doctrines and worship ; to which all gave marked attention. The whole scene is strikingly dramatic. "At the Colloquy of Poissy," remarks a spirit essayist, " Beza stands before us full of stateliness and dignity; while the Reformation assumes its most imposing attitude." † The grave and massive proportions of Protestantism loom up with grandeur against this background of priestly pomp and courtly elegance, as we contemplate the Reformers forgetting even the presence of royalty, in abasement at the footstool of God. ‡

Those admirable forms of prayer for morning

* Beza, *Histoire Ecclésiastique*, tom. i., p. 502.

† Sayous, *Etudes Littéraires sur les Ecrivains Français de la Réformation*, tom. i., p. 290.

‡ The fact of its use by Beza on this conspicuous occasion, has led some to ascribe the authorship of the Confession of Sins to that Reformer. But we have elsewhere furnished sufficient evidence that this prayer already existed as a part of the Calvinistic Liturgy; having been composed and *published* as early as 1543, that is, eighteen years prior to the date of the Colloquy of Poissy.

and evening worship, which we have elsewhere
quoted from Calvin, connect themselves closely
in our mind with a reminiscence of one of the
most illustrious characters of Huguenot times,—
the excellent Coligny. An interesting picture of
the daily habits of this remarkable man is given by
a contemporary writer. " As soon as he had risen
from his bed early in the morning, having knelt
down with all his household, he prayed according to the Form commonly employed in the French
Churches. After which, waiting for the hour of
the sermon, which came twice a day, once with
the singing of Psalms, he gave audience to the
deputies of the churches who were sent to him,
or attended to public business, which he yet continued to discuss a little after the sermon, till the
dinner hour. Standing near the table when it
was set, with his wife by his side, they sang a
psalm, and then asked the ordinary blessing. All
this an infinite number of captains and colonels,
not only French, but German also, can bear witness that he was accustomed to observe without
omission, from day to day; not only in the quiet
of his family, but also in the army.* The cloth

* The Huguenot army was subjected to severe religious discipline.
" Besides the ordinary exhortations and prayers," says Theodore Beza,

removed, rising with his attendants, he returned thanks himself, or by his minister. The same he practised at supper; and seeing that his household were inconvenienced by the lateness of the evening prayer, he directed each to be present at the close of the supper, when, after singing of psalms, there was prayer. It is impossible to give the number of those among the French nobility who established in their families this religious discipline of the Admiral."*

It was in the act of repeating the Morning Prayer of Calvin's Liturgy, that the last moments of Coligny's life was spent. Early on the fatal morning of St. Bartholomew's day, 1572, the Admiral, who was then confined to his bed by the wound he had received from an assassin two days before, sent for his chaplain to engage with him in the customary devotions. While following the familiar words thus uttered, he was attacked by the band of murderers who burst into his room, and dispatched him with their daggers.

"they attended general prayers, especially at six o'clock in the morning; at the close of which, ministers and people, without exception, went to work upon the fortifications with all their might; all returning again at four o'clock to prayer.—*Hist. Ecclés.*, tom. ii., p. 162.

* *Mémoires de Coligny;* compiled, it is presumed, by Cornaton, a faithful servant of the Admiral. Quoted by DE FELICE, pp. 102, 103.

Thus died Coligny. Even so have we seen John Knox, with the like holy joy, though on a tranquil death-bed, listening to the rehearsal of Calvin's Evening Prayer.*

Clustered around these forms of worship are a thousand similar recollections of bloodshed and oppression. Those fearful massacres which so often devastated the churches of the Reformation in France, even while as yet they maintained a species of legal existence, being partially tolerated by law, are vividly brought before us as we survey these prayers and services. For it was most frequently while engaged in their celebration, that the Huguenots were surprised and overwhelmed by their merciless foes. So at Vassy, in February, 1562, when the Protestants had assembled in a barn to the number of twelve hundred, to celebrate the LORD's Supper. The Duke of Guise with a band of soldiers arrived, surrounded the place, burst in upon the assembly, and slaughtered as many as they could reach.† Not less barbarous was the assault upon Châtaigneraie in 1595; when the Leaguers fell suddenly on a congregation while attending Divine service, and cruelly murdered two hundred per-

* *Vide* p. 64.   † BEZA, *Histoire Ecclésiastique.*

sons of all ages. Among the victims was a babe just presented for baptism, whose life-stream was poured forth before the symbol of regeneration touched his forehead.*

Such instances might be adduced in multitudes. The Liturgy of French Protestantism has been bathed with the blood of its martyrs. What wonder that it should commend itself to the reverence and love of their descendants? No Church has suffered like that of the Huguenots, and none has transmitted to our day more touching memories, attached to such precious relics.

We may be allowed to vary these souvenirs by adducing one of a more lively cast. It is connected with the baptismal service. When the famous Claude was pastor of the church at Charenton, near Paris (about the middle of the seventeenth century), he was called on one occasion to perform the marriage ceremony between two Huguenots in high life; of whom the bridegroom was a decrepit septuagenarian, leading to the altar a young girl of some sixteen summers. As the minister saw this ill-matched couple advancing up the aisle to meet him, whether by accident or design we cannot say, he opened his

* DE FELICE, p. 271.

book to the baptismal form, and addressed the disconcerted bridegroom with the interrogation: "Dost thou here present this child to be baptized?"

In those fortified cities where the Reformed were able for a while to maintain a footing, they continued to observe in a public and official manner the rites of worship. Among the registers of the ancient Protestant town of Montauban, are preserved two interesting prayers which were used in the seventeenth century, at the opening and close of the sessions of the civic council. The following is a translation.[*]

In the Name of God:

PRAYER AT THE OPENING OF THE COUNCIL.

Almighty and eternal GOD: We beseech thee, for the sake of JESUS CHRIST, thy Son our Lord, to regard us with thy grace and favour; and by thy Holy Spirit to preside among us as we are here assembled. Guide and conduct us in all things that concern the government of this city, for which thy providence hath brought us together.

---

[*] These prayers are given in the *Bulletin de la Société de l'Histoire du Protestantisme Français*, Avril, 1853, p. 486.

Endue us with the spirit of wisdom, fully to execute thy sovereign will, to deliberate and to resolve only as shall promote thine honour and glory, in the welfare and preservation of ourselves and our fellow-citizens. Through JESUS CHRIST thy Son our Lord. Amen.

THANKSGIVING AT THE CLOSE OF THE COUNCIL.

O GOD! who dispensest thy gifts to men, that they may acknowledge and praise thee in them: We give thee thanks for thy gracious help in our present transactions. And since thou only art mighty to accomplish and perfect whatever may seem good in thy sight: Most humbly we beseech thee of thy good pleasure to make us willing and able to carry out those measures which have been here determined; that each of us, according to his office and calling, may faithfully, constantly, and diligently labour for thy glory, the good and comfort of all men in this city, and our final salvation: Through JESUS CHRIST thy Son our Lord. Amen.*

---

* It is pleasing to find on the first leaf of the ancient records of the city of "New Amsterdam" a similar form of Prayer, which was in use about the middle of the seventeenth century.—See VALENTINE'S *History of New York*, pp. 55—57.

When, after the revocation of the Edict of
Nantes, the Reformed congregations were deprived of every vestige of freedom, and dispersed
to the wilderness and the mountains for refuge,
we should expect to see them forsaking those
rites which they no longer had opportunity of
observing in a quiet and regular manner.   Instead
of this, the contrary is true.   With stronger
attachment than ever, the churches of the Desert
clung to their venerated forms.   Even the ex-
cited bands of the Camisards in the South were
accustomed to celebrate with regularity their ancient services.*   " The worship of the Desert,"
says the historian, " was the same as in times of
freedom : liturgical prayers, the singing of psalms,
preaching, and the administration of the LORD's
Supper on feast-days ;† a simple worship, easily
performed everywhere, and which demanded no
more preparation than that of the upper chamber
where the apostles and first Christians of Jeru-
salem assembled.   This simplicity had, moreover,
something grand and noble.   The calm of the

* DE FELICE, p. 436.
† These feast-days were the three great festivals retained by the
Reformed Churches : the days of our LORD's Nativity and Resurrection, and the season of Pentecost. A fourth sacramental occasion was
(and is still) observed on the first Sunday of September.

solitude suddenly broken by the voice of prayer; the songs of the faithful ascending to the Invisible One amid the beauties of nature; the minister of CHRIST, like the believers of the Primitive Church, invoking his GOD in behalf of oppressors who were enraged that they could not yet drag him to the scaffold; poor peasants, humble labourers, laying aside for a day their implements of toil, more anxious for the sublime interests of faith and the life to come; a common apprehension of danger, that kept their souls continually in the presence of the Sovereign Judge: all this gave to the assemblies of the Desert an imposing majesty harmonizing well with the teachings of the Gospel."*

We have spoken of the French Psalm-book as closely connected with the Liturgy of Calvin. In fact, these two formularies were invariably bound up together. It has been the good fortune of the Church of France to possess from the outset an excellent metrical version of the Psalms; which, at once received into general use, became one of the most attractive features of the Reformation. "They sung," says the old writer we have before quoted, "Psalms in French rhyme, with vocal and instrumental music, which extremely pleased

* DE FELICE, p. 452.

such people as were fond of novelty, and contributed to increase their numbers daily."* These sacred poems, with the simple and appropriate melodies to which they were set, readily finding place in the memory of the faithful, became the language of their devotion, their consolation in trial, their rejoicing in success, their watchword at all times. An incident in the religious wars of the Huguenots illustrates this fact. When the town of Montauban, which had been for many years their stronghold, was besieged in 1623, all attempt to capture it proved ineffectual. At length it was determined to raise the siege. On the evening before this purpose was put in execution, "the people of the town were apprized of the approaching decampment of the army, by a Protestant soldier, who played upon his flute the air of the sixty-eighth Psalm.† The besieged took

* CASTELNAU, *Memoirs*, etc., p. 125.

† This Psalm, one of the most stirring compositions of the kind, was the war-song of the Camisards, raised whenever they went forth to battle. The first verse, which was the part used on such occasions, may be thus translated :—

> Let God but rise and show his face,
> And in a moment from the place
>   Our foes are disappearing.
> Their camp dispersed, bereft their pride,
> Astonished, pressed on every side,
>   They flee at his appearing.

this for the signal of their deliverance, and were not mistaken.*

" Ah ! how they penetrate the very soul at such moments," exclaims a brilliant delineator of the Huguenot character, " these rude songs of our forefathers ! These psalms are our epic ; and the most profoundly truthful epic that has ever been written or sung by any nation ; an endless work, of which each of us becomes afresh the author ; a sacred treasure, where are gathered beside our patriotic remembrances, the remembrances, hopes, joys, and griefs of each. Not a verse, not a line, which is not a whole history, or a whole poem. This was sung by a mother at the cradle of her first-born ; that was chanted by one of our martyrs as he marched to his death. There is the song of the Vaudois returning armed to their country ; here that of the Camisards advancing to battle. This was the line interrupted by a ball ; this was half murmured by an expiring father, who went to finish it among the angels. O our psalms !

> We shall behold their scattered tents
> Fade like a vapour dark and dense,
>   Their nothingness resuming :
> As melts the wax in fervent heat,
> So melt the wicked when they meet
>   Our God, their strength consuming.

* DE FELICE, p. 304.

our psalms! Who in human language could ever
tell what you say to us in our solitudes, upon the
soil crimsoned with our blood, and under the vault
of heaven, from whose height look down upon
us those who with us have wept, sung, and
prayed!"*

Yes, "*sung and prayed;*" the halo of this ancient worship robes the prayers of these illustrious
witnesses of GOD with not less brightness than
their songs of praise. No psalm thrills more
powerfully on the ear of the worshipper than
that beautiful Confession of Sins, which, in the
language of another, ascends as a fragrant incense
on every Sabbath day, from every " temple " on
the soil of France.† No psalm is fraught with
recollections more vivid and touching, than are
connected with that prayer of consecration by
which the aged Rabaut, the pastor of the Desert,
inducted his only son to a ministry of toil and
martyrdom.‡ No psalm comes up in more pathetic

* *The Priest and the Huguenot*, by L. BUNGENER, one of the most
delightful of historic illustrations, vol. i., pp. 141, 142. An excellent translation has made this work known and popular among us.
Boston: Gould and Lincoln, 1854.

† Rev. PHILIPPE BOUCHER, in an address before the General
Assembly of the Church of Scotland.

‡ DE FELICE, p. 545. The scene is described with intense interest
by BUNGENER, in the last pages of his remarkable work. *The Priest
and the Huguenot*, vol. ii., ch. xcix.

strains to our memory, than those morning and evening prayers, and those communion forms, in the use of which Calvin, and Knox, and Coligny, breathed their souls away to GOD.

Never, we sincerely trust, will the day come when, by any adventitious influence of "new light" and new fashion, the Churches of France shall be persuaded to violate the sanctity of these venerable psalms and prayers, either by introduction of fancied improvements, or by exchange for novelties of the day. The hasty concoctions of modern innovators could scarcely supply the place which these formularies are entitled to occupy in the affections of every worshipper who adopts them, and in the reverence of all others.

V.

John Knox and the Church of Scotland.

"Ceremonies grounded upon GOD'S word, and approved in the New Testament, are commendable, as the Circumstance thereof doth support. Those that man hath invented, though he had never so good Occasion thereunto, if they be once abused, import a necessity, hinder GOD'S Word, or be drawn into a Superstition, without respect ought to be abolished."—PREFACE TO THE BOOK OF COMMON ORDER.

PERHAPS no one of the great Reformers was better fitted than JOHN KNOX to prepare forms of worship for the Churches of the Reformation. In him a temperament naturally enthusiastic was heightened by the ardour of religious zeal; and the courage that "knew not what it was to quail before the face of man," consisted with a pious reverence that abased him in the presence of GOD. These qualities alone would insure earnest and holy praying, and secure its prevalence at the throne of grace; but in John Knox, their usefulness to the Church was enhanced by a gift of utterance seldom equalled without a special inspiration. Vehement of thought, and fluent of expression, his oratory and his devotions were alike distinguished for striking and felicitous language. A deep experience of the Christian life, and a wide acquaintance with it in others, enabled him largely to represent the wants and feelings of worshippers, in those forms of supplication which he drew up for their use.

Thus much would be pronounced by any one at all familiar with the writings of Knox, however ignorant of the services he actually rendered to religious worship. The fervent spirit of the man breathes in every page of his works. On first perusing them, we could not but wish that the great Reformer might have left us some fruits of his singular gift of prayer, beyond those which are to be found scattered among his treatises and letters.

And here let me cite as a specimen one of those prayers which occur among the writings of this Reformer. I select the following, not for its greater merit, but for its brevity, as more suited to the purpose. It is taken from the conclusion of one of his treatises, and in the original is entitled,

A GODLY PRAYER.

O LORD, most strong and mighty GOD! Who destroyest the counsels of the ungodly, and at thy pleasure riddest away the tyrants of this world, so that no force can resist thine everlasting determination: We, thy poor creatures and humble servants, do most earnestly desire thee, for the love thou hast to thy well-beloved only-begotten Son, our Lord and Saviour JESUS CHRIST, that thou wilt look upon thy cause;—for it is time, O LORD!—and bring to nought all those things that are, or shall be appointed, determined, and agreed against thee and thy holy word. Let not the enemies of thy truth too miserably oppress thy word and thy servants which seek thy glory, tender* the advancement of thy pure religion, and above all things wish in their heart that thy holy name alone may be glorified among all nations. Give unto the mouth of thy people truth and wisdom which no man may resist. And although we have most justly deserved this plague and famine of thy word, yet, upon our true repentance, grant, we beseech thee, we may be thereof released. And here we promise, before thy Divine Majesty, better to use thy gifts than we have done, and more straightly to order our lives according to thy holy will and pleasure. And we will sing

---

* *Tender*, i. e., regard with kindness.

perpetual praises to thy most blessed name, world without end, through JESUS CHRIST our Lord. Amen.*

That there were some qualities, however, in the Scottish Reformer's character, wanting to a perfect adaptedness for the work of devotional writing, we are free to acknowledge. The delicacy, the tenderness that should deal with certain phases of religious experience, that should express certain emotions of the soul: of these, though not destitute, neither was he remarkably possessed. Nor might we reasonably look to him for these. Knox was a man raised up to do battle in fierce times, with rude and rough adversaries; and though not without kindly sympathies and gentle susceptibilities, he was not so placed as to develope them in full proportion with other attributes of his noble soul. But the worship of the Church of Scotland did not suffer by this deficiency in the author of its forms. Happily for Knox, on this and other accounts, he came early in his apostolic career, under the benign irradiation of a clear and beautiful mind, adorned

* See the Writings of JOHN KNOX, published by the Presbyterian Board, Philadelphia.

with some of the graces in which himself was wanting: the mind of CALVIN.*

In the year 1554, finding it no longer safe to remain in Scotland, where the Protestant cause was suffering violence under the reign of Mary, Knox repaired to Geneva, a place where he already had many friends and well-wishers among his Reformed brethren. By Calvin he was received with open arms; and in the intimate society of that remarkable man, he passed much time. With occasional absences, during one of which he visited the English refugees at Frankfort, and during another returned for some months to Scotland, Knox spent parts of six years in the city of Geneva, dwelling in the bosom of his own family, pursuing various studies under the direction of his illustrious master, and having charge of a

* " The world has been accustomed to impute a stoic coldness and severity to his character, but the whole tenor of his life contradicts this imputation. The deep feeling for, and knowledge of, the sufferings of others, which he derived from his own experience, and which was not dulled in his old age, are exemplified by a variety of instances. Passages occur even in the 'Institutes,' which prove his gentleness of spirit, his sympathy with mankind, and knowledge of the human heart. There was nothing stern, formal, or repulsive in his manners. Women never shrank from frequent or familiar conversation with him on subjects of religion. And that which will say still more in his favour, his colleagues in office often spoke, after his death, in terms of the highest praise, of his gentleness, and agreeable, loving temper."—HENRY's *Life of Calvin*, i. 278.

small congregation of English exiles, who like him had fled to the capital of the Protestant world. The greatest affection united him with the members of his little flock; and he was happy in the friendship of Calvin and other pastors of Geneva. So much was he delighted with the purity of religion established in that city, that he warmly recommended it to his religious acquaintances in England, as the best Christian asylum to which they could flee. "In my heart," says he, in a letter to a friend, "I could have wished, yea, and cannot cease to wish, that it might please God to guide and conduct yourself to this place; where, I neither fear nor am ashamed to say, is the most perfect school of Christ that ever was in the earth since the days of the apostles. In other places, I confess Christ to be truly preached; but manners and religion to be so sincerely reformed, I have not yet seen in any other place beside."*

As on all important points of faith and discipline these great Reformers perfectly agreed, so, too, in respect to forms of public worship their practice was harmonious. Calvin, as we have

* M'Crie's *Life of Knox*, period V.

H

already seen, had ten years before the arrival of Knox inaugurated the Reformed service in the Churches of Geneva; according to the mode and manner which he deemed most agreeable to the word of GOD and primitive custom. Knox, in his Letter of Instruction written from Geneva to the Protestants of Scotland, takes for the model of his directions that Liturgy which he finds in use among his Genevan brethren, and recommends the same general order to be observed in their assemblies. For beauty of thought and propriety of counsel, this letter deserves quotation. "Your beginning," says the Reformer, "should be by confessing of your offences, and invocation of the Spirit of the Lord JESUS to assist you in all your godly enterprises. And then let some place of Scripture be plainly and distinctly read, as much as shall be thought sufficient for a day or time. In reading the Scriptures, I would ye should join some books of the Old and some of the New Testament together, as Genesis and one of the Evangelists, Exodus with another, and so forth; ever ending such books as ye begin, as the time will suffer; for it shall greatly comfort you to hear that harmony and well-tuned song of the Holy Spirit speaking in our fathers from the

beginning. It shall confirm you in these dangerous and perilous days to behold the face of CHRIST
JESUS, and his loving spouse and Church, from
Abel to himself, and from himself to this day, in
all ages to be one. Like as your assemblies ought
to begin, with confession and invocation of GOD's
Holy Spirit, so would I that they never finished
without thanksgiving, and common prayers for
princes, rulers, and magistrates; for the liberty
and free passage of CHRIST's Gospel; for the
comfort and deliverance of our afflicted brethren
in all places now persecuted, but most cruelly
within the realm of France and England; and
for such other things as the Spirit of the Lord
JESUS shall teach you to be profitable either to
yourselves, or yet to your brethren, wheresoever
they are."*

The necessities of the English Church at Frankfort, to which Knox ministered for a short time,
led him in 1554 to draw up an Order of Worship,
closely modelled upon the Genevan service.†

---

* KNOX, *A most Godly Counsel*, etc.

† See "A Brief Discourse of the Troubles begun at Frankfort in
Germany, A. D. 1554, about the Book of Common Prayer and Ceremonies." First published 1575. Reprinted in "The Phenix; or, a
Revival of Scarce and Valuable Pieces from the Remotest Antiquity,
down to the Present Times." London, 1707.

When, after a short stay at Frankfort, the Reformer went back to Geneva, and took charge of the English congregation in that city, this form was unanimously adopted, and in February, 1556, was published.* The design of its publication was not simply to supply the wants of the congregation at Geneva, but rather, as we learn from the Preface, with a view to its extensive use in England and Scotland. And upon the return of Knox to Scotland, he obtained the general adherence of the Scottish churches to this Order. It was adopted by Act of the General Assembly as early as 1560,† and in subsequent years repeatedly approved, as the established form of worship.

"We, therefore," says the Preface to the Book of Common Order, dated at Geneva, in February, 1556, "not as the greatest clerks of all, but as the least able of many, do present unto you, which desire the increase of God's Glory, and the pure Simplicity of his Word, a Form and Order of a Reformed Church, limit within the Compass of God's

---

* The title of this book, as subsequently reprinted (in 1600), was, "The Book of Common Order, or the Order of the English Kirk at Geneva, whereof John Knox was Minister: Approved by the famous and learned man, John Calvin. Received and used by the Reformed Kirk of Scotland, and ordinarily prefixed to the Psalms in Metre."— DUNLOP'S Confessions, ii. 383.

† The First Book of Discipline, 1560.

Word, which our Saviour hath left unto us as only
sufficient to govern all our actions by.—And also,
knowing that negligence in reforming that Religion which was begun in England, was not the
least cause of GOD's Rod laid upon us, having
now obtained, by the merciful Providence of our
heavenly Father, a free Church for all our nation
in this most worthy City of Geneva, we presented
to the judgment of the famous man, John Calvin,
and others learned in these Parts, the Order
which we minded to use in our Church; who
approving it as sufficient for a Christian Congregation, we put the same in Execution, nothing
doubting but all godly men shall be much edified
thereby."*

It was not designed that the use of these prayers
should be confined to the services of the Sabbath.
The Church of Scotland, in the early days of the
Reformation, enjoined more frequent celebration
of Divine Service. It recommended that where
practicable, and especially " in great towns, there
be either Sermon or Common Prayers, with some
Exercise of reading of Scriptures, every day."†

* THE PREFACE: " *To our Brethren in England and elsewhere,
which love Jesus Christ unfeignedly.*"—DUNLOP'S *Confessions*, ii. 385.
† *The First Book of Discipline,* ch. xi.—When Mr. Robert Bruce

On Sundays, besides the service of prayer and preaching in the morning, there was a catechetical exercise for the young in the afternoon. On one day of the week, also, was held a meeting, for free and familiar exposition of the Scriptures; in which "every man had Liberty to utter and declare his mind and knowledge to the Comfort and Consolation of the Kirk."* These exercises, answering precisely to our meetings for conference and prayer, were termed more scripturally by our fathers, "prophesyings," or "interpretations." † The LORD's Supper was administered four times a year. ‡

These facts enable us to form some idea of the arrangements for public worship, which our Reformers attempted to provide in all the Churches

was relegated to Inverness, A. D. 1605, he "remained there four years, teaching every Sabbath before noon, and every Wednesday, and *exercised at the reading of the prayers every other night.*"—CALDERWOOD, p. 496.

* *The First Book of Discipline*, ch. xii.

† The practice was borrowed, as we have seen, from the Genevan Church: it was adopted very generally in the Church of England also, and remained until arbitrarily broken up by Queen Elizabeth. —See *Memoirs of Archbp. Grindal.*

‡ In 1711, the General Assembly recommended to the Presbyteries a more frequent celebration of the LORD's Supper: "that it be duly observed in their bounds through the several months in the year;" but it does not appear that this action was followed up.—See *Compendium of the Laws of the Church of Scotland*, Part Second, p. 164.

of Scotland. That they succeeded in establishing them everywhere, we have no reason to believe. But in many places, the scheme was carried out. In many towns and villages, the church-going bell was to be heard, not alone upon the Sabbath, but often, or even daily, through the week. The church was regarded, not simply as a place of weekly congregation, but as a sanctuary and asylum, always open to the solitary worshipper, who sought opportunity of quiet devotion. Frequently, too, was opportunity afforded of hearing the word read, and uniting with the assembly of the faithful in the hymn of praise and the voice of prayer. We love to look back on those days of open churches and daily worship. There were prevalent sins and errors in those days; ignorance and superstition yet remained to be rooted out; but in the measures adopted for their eradication, and the promoting of truth and godliness, we discover wisdom and judiciousness, unrestrained by the fear of infringing on established custom, or offending unconquerable prejudice.

We proceed to give the form of Divine Service appointed in the Scottish Order of Worship, for the morning of the LORD's Day.

THE ORDER OF PUBLIC WORSHIP.

When the congregation is assembled at the hour appointed, the minister useth one of these two confessions, or like in effect, exhorting the people diligently to examine themselves, following in their hearts the tenor of his words.

THE CONFESSION OF OUR SINS.

O Eternal God, and most merciful Father! We confess and acknowledge here before thy Divine Majesty, that we are miserable sinners, conceived and born in sin and iniquity, so that in us there is no goodness. For the flesh evermore rebelleth against the spirit; whereby we continually transgress thine holy precepts and commandments, and so purchase to ourselves, through thy just judgment, death and condemnation. Notwithstanding, O Heavenly Father, forasmuch as we are displeased with ourselves for the sins that we have committed against thee, and do unfeignedly repent us of the same: we most humbly beseech thee, for Jesus Christ's sake, to show thy mercy upon us, to forgive us all our sins, and to increase thine Holy Spirit in us; that we, acknowledging from the bottom of our hearts our

own unrighteousness, may from henceforth not
only mortify our sinful lusts and affections, but
also bring forth such fruits as may be agreeable
to thy most blessed will; not for the worthiness
thereof, but for the merits of thy dearly beloved
Son JESUS CHRIST, our only Saviour, whom thou
hast already given an oblation and offering for
our sins, and for whose sake we are certainly persuaded that thou wilt deny us nothing that we
shall ask in his Name according to thy will. For
thy Holy Spirit doth assure our consciences that
thou art our merciful Father, and so lovest us,
thy children, through him, that nothing is able
to remove thine heavenly grace and favour from
us. To thee, therefore, O Father, with the Son
and with the Holy Ghost, be all honour and glory,
world without end. Amen.

ANOTHER CONFESSION OF SINS.

Almighty GOD, we are unworthy to come into
thy presence, by reason of our manifold sins and
wickedness; much less to receive any grace or
mercy at thine hands, if thou shouldst deal with
us according to our deservings. For we have
sinned, O LORD, against thee, and have offended
thy holy Majesty. We were conceived in sin,

and in iniquity was every one of us born. All the days of our life we have continued in sin and wickedness, to follow the corruption of our fleshly nature. Therefore, O LORD, if thou shouldst enter into judgment with us, just occasion hast thou not only to punish these our mortal bodies, but also to punish us both in body and soul eternally, if thou shouldst deal with us according to the rigour of thy justice. But yet, O LORD, as we acknowledge our sins and offences, together with the fearful judgment that justly, by reason thereof, thou mayst pour upon us: so also, we acknowledge thee to be a merciful GOD, a loving and a favourable Father, to all them that unfeignedly turn unto thee. Wherefore, O LORD, we thy people, the workmanship of thine own hands, most humbly beseech thee, for CHRIST thy Son's sake, to show thy mercy upon us, and forgive us all our offences. Impute not unto us the sins of our youth, neither yet receive thou a reckoning of us for the iniquity of our old age. But as thou hast showed thyself merciful to all them that have truly called unto thee, so show the like favour unto us thy poor servants. Endue our hearts, O GOD, with such a true and perfect acknowledging of our sins, that we may pour forth before thee the unfeigned sighs of our troubled hearts and afflicted consciences for our offences committed against thee.   Inflame our souls with such zeal and fervency towards thy glory, that all the days of our life our only study and labour may be to serve and worship thee, in spirit and in truth.   Preserve us from all impediments that in anywise may hinder us; but especially from the craft of Satan, from the snares of the world, and from the naughty lusts and affections of the flesh.   Make thy Spirit, O God, once to take such full possession of our hearts, that not only the actions of our life, but also the words of our mouth, and the least thought of our mind, may be guided and ruled thereby.

And finally, grant that all our time may be so spent in thy true fear and obedience, that we may end the same in the sanctification of thy blessed name, through Jesus Christ our Lord; to whom, with thee and the Holy Ghost, be all honour and glory, both now and for ever.   Amen.

This done, the people sing a Psalm all together, in a plain tune; which ended, the minister prayeth for the assistance of God's Holy Spirit, as the same shall move his heart, and so proceedeth to

*the sermon, using after the sermon this prayer
following, or such like.*

A PRAYER FOR THE WHOLE ESTATE OF CHRIST'S CHURCH.

Almighty GOD and most merciful Father, we
humbly submit ourselves, and fall down before
thy Majesty, beseeching thee, from the bottom of
our hearts, that this seed of thy word, now sown
among us, may take such deep root, that neither
the burning heat of persecution cause it to wither,
neither the thorny cares of this life do choke it,
but that, as seed sown in good ground, it may
bring forth thirty, sixty, and an hundred fold, as
thine heavenly wisdom hath appointed.   And
because we have need continually to crave many
things at thine hands, we humbly beseech thee,
O heavenly Father, to grant us thine Holy Spirit
to direct our petitions, that they may proceed
from such a fervent mind as may be agreeable to
thy most blessed will.   And seeing that our in-
firmity is able to do nothing without thine help,
and that thou art not ignorant with how many
and great temptations we poor wretches are on
every side enclosed and compassed, let thy strength,
O LORD, sustain our weakness, that we, being

defended with the force of thy grace, may be safely preserved against all assaults of Satan, who goeth about continually like a roaring lion, seeking to devour us. Increase our faith, O merciful Father, that we do not swerve at any time from thine heavenly word; but augment in us hope and love, with a careful keeping of all thy commandments, that no hardness of heart, no hypocrisy, no concupiscence of the eyes, nor enticements of the world, do draw us away from thine obedience. And seeing we live now in these most perilous times, let thy Fatherly providence defend us against the violence of all our enemies, who do everywhere pursue us; but chiefly against the wicked rage and furious uproars of that Romish idol and enemy to thy CHRIST.

Furthermore, forasmuch as by thine holy apostle we are taught to make our prayers and supplications for all men, we pray not only for ourselves here present, but beseech thee also to reduce all such as yet be ignorant from the miserable captivity of blindness and error to the pure understanding of thine heavenly truth: that we all, with one consent and unity of mind, may worship thee our only GOD and Saviour; and that all pastors, shepherds, and ministers, to whom thou hast committed the dispensation of thine holy word, and charge of thy chosen people, may both in their life and doctrine be found faithful, setting only before their eyes thy glory; and that by them all poor sheep which wander and go astray may be gathered and brought home to thy fold.

Moreover, because the hearts of rulers are in thine hands, we beseech thee to direct and govern the hearts of all kings, princes, and magistrates, to whom thou hast committed the sword; especially, O LORD, according to our bounden duty, we beseech thee to maintain and increase the noble estate of the Queen's Majesty, and her honourable council, with all the estate and whole body of the commonwealth. Let thy fatherly favour so preserve her, and thine Holy Spirit so govern her heart, that she may in such sort execute her office that thy religion may be purely maintained, manners reformed, and sin punished, according to the precise rule of thine holy word.

And for that we be all members of the mystical body of CHRIST JESUS, we make our requests unto thee, O heavenly Father, for all such as are afflicted with any kind of cross or tribulation, as war, plague, famine, sickness, poverty, imprison-

ment, persecution, banishment, or any other kind
of thy chastisements, whether it be grief of body
or unquietness of mind; that it would please thee
to give them patience and constancy, till thou
send them full deliverance out of all their troubles.
And, finally, O LORD GOD, most merciful Father,
we most humbly beseeeh thee to show thy great
mercies upon those our brethren who are persecuted, cast in prison, and daily condemned to
death, for the testimony of thy truth: and though
they be utterly destitute of all man's aid, yet let
thy sweet comfort never depart from them, but
so inflame their hearts with thine Holy Spirit,
that they may boldly and cheerfully abide such
trial as thy godly wisdom shall appoint; so that
at length, as well by their death as by their life,
the kingdom of thy Son JESUS CHRIST may increase and shine through all the world; in whose
name we make our humble petitions unto thee, as
he hath taught us, saying,

Our Father, which art in heaven, hallowed be
thy name. Thy kingdom come. Thy will be done
on earth, as it is in heaven. Give us this day
our daily bread. And forgive us our debts, as we
forgive our debtors. And lead us not into temptation, but deliver us from evil. For thine is the

kingdom, and the power, and the glory, for ever. Amen.

Almighty and everlasting GOD, vouchsafe, we beseech thee, to grant us perfect continuance in the lively faith, augmenting the same in us daily, till we grow to the full measure of our perfection in CHRIST, whereof we make our confession, saying,

I believe in GOD the Father Almighty, Maker of heaven and earth; and in JESUS CHRIST his only Son our Lord, who was conceived by the Holy Ghost, born of the Virgin Mary, suffered under Pontius Pilate, was crucified, dead and buried; He descended into hell; the third day He rose again from the dead; He ascended into heaven, and sitteth on the right hand of GOD the Father Almighty; from thence He shall come to judge the quick and the dead. I believe in the Holy Ghost; the holy Catholic Church; the communion of saints; the forgiveness of sins; the resurrection of the body, and the life everlasting. Amen.

Then the people sing a psalm; which ended, the minister pronounceth one of these blessings, and so the congregation departeth.

The LORD bless us, and save us; the LORD make his face to shine upon us, and be merciful unto us; the LORD turn his countenance towards us, and grant us his peace.

The grace of our Lord JESUS CHRIST, the love of GOD, and the communion of the Holy Ghost, be with you all. Amen.*

A GODLY PRAYER, TO BE SAID AT ALL TIMES.

HONOUR and praise be given to thee, O LORD GOD Almighty, most dear Father of heaven, for all thy mercies and loving-kindness showed unto us, in that it hath pleased thy gracious goodness freely and of thine own accord to elect and choose us to salvation before the beginning of the world.

---

* *It shall not be necessary for the minister daily to repeat all these things before mentioned, but, beginning with some manner of confession, to proceed to the sermon; which being ended, he either useth the prayer for all estates before mentioned, or else prayeth as the Spirit of God shall move his heart, framing the same according to the time and matter which he hath intreated of. And if there shall be at any time any present plague, famine, pestilence, war, or such like, which be evident tokens of God's wrath, as it is our part to acknowledge our sins to be the occasion thereof, so are we appointed by the Scriptures to give ourselves to mourning, fasting, and prayer, as the means to turn away God's heavy displeasure. Therefore it shall be convenient that the minister at such time do not only admonish the people thereof, but also use some form of prayer according as the present necessity requireth; to the which he may appoint, by a common consent, some several day after the sermon weekly to be observed.*

And even like continual thanks be given to thee for creating us after thine own image; for redeeming us with the precious blood of thy dear Son, when we were utterly lost; for sanctifying us with thine Holy Spirit in the revelation and knowledge of thine holy word; for helping and succouring us in all our needs and necessities; for saving us from all dangers of body and soul; for comforting us so fatherly in all our tribulations and persecutions; for sparing us so long, and giving us so large a time of repentance. These benefits, O most merciful Father, like as we acknowledge to have received of thine only goodness, even so we beseech thee, for thy dear Son JESUS CHRIST's sake, to grant us always thine Holy Spirit, whereby we may continually grow in thankfulness towards thee, and be led into all truth, and comforted in all our adversities. O LORD, strengthen our faith; kindle it more in ferventness and love towards thee, and our neighbours, for thy sake.   Suffer us not, most dear Father, to receive thy word any more in vain; but grant us always the assistance of thy grace and Holy Spirit, that in heart, word, and deed, we may sanctify and do worship to thy name.

Help to amplify and increase thy kingdom;

that whatsoever thou sendest, we may be heartily well content with thy good pleasure and will. Let us not lack the thing, O Father! without the which we cannot serve thee; but bless thou so all the works of our hands, that we may have sufficient, and not be chargeable, but rather helpful unto others. Be merciful, O LORD, to our offences; and seeing our debt is great, which thou hast forgiven us in JESUS CHRIST, make us to love thee and our neighbours so much the more. Be thou our Father, our Captain and Defender in all temptations; hold thou us by thy merciful hand; that we may be delivered from all inconveniences, and end our lives in the sanctifying and honouring of thine holy name, through JESUS CHRIST our Lord and only Saviour. Amen.

Let thy mighty hand and outstretched arm, O LORD, be still our defence; thy mercy and lovingkindness in JESUS CHRIST, thy dear Son, our salvation; thy true and holy word our instruction; thy grace and Holy Spirit our comfort and consolation, unto the end and in the end. Amen.

O LORD, increase our faith. Amen.

VI.

The First Sacrament in Scotland.

"There is no warrantable form [of celebrating the LORD'S Supper] directed or approven by the Kirk, besides that which is extant in print before the Psalm Book; according to which, as I have always done, I now minister that sacrament."—A SCOTTISH CLERGYMAN IN 1620.

In a hall of the ancient baronial house of Calder, West Lothian, there hangs a portrait of John Knox, with this inscription: "The first Sacrament of the Supper given in Scotland after the Reformation, was dispensed in this hall."*

It seems probable that the occasion to which this language refers, if not actually the earliest celebration of that ordinance in Scotland, was the first after Knox's return from Geneva, in August, 1555. Then, by the persuasion of our Reformer, the adherents of the Protestant faith, who had hitherto compromised with Popery so far as to attend mass for the sake of appearances, were led to an open breach with Rome; and from this period may, in some sense, be dated the public manifestation of the Reformed movement in Scotland.

* M'CRIE'S *Life of Knox*, p. 118, *note*.

This, too, was the first administration of the LORD's Supper by John Knox, according to the form and manner which he had seen practised at Geneva, and which afterwards became the appointed order of administration in the Church of Scotland.

It needs no vivid fancy to picture a scene of striking interest, as occurring under these circumstances at that sacramental season in Calderhouse. Standing behind the sacred table was the venerable figure of the Reformer, small in stature, but not without dignity of bearing, and a gravity of aspect increased by the length of the flowing beard, which reached almost to his waist. His pallid, sickly countenance is lighted up by the fire of a keen, penetrating eye; as, in uttering the exhortations of the communion form, he looks around him on the small but crowded company who are collected in that hall. Some of these are men of no mean fame. Observe, as he goes up to receive the holy emblems, the young Lord James Stuart, now in his twenty-second year; destined at no distant day to assume the regency of the kingdom, as the famous Earl of Murray. Already, in sternness of temperament and austerity of manners, that savour of his priestly education, he resembles not a little his admired and beloved master. Now, the young Lord Erskine advances to the table; a gallant nobleman, of free and generous soul, upon whom the honours of the regency will also devolve, but whose gentle spirit will break under the trials of troublous times.* Next comes another youth, the future Earl of Argyle: a faithful disciple and ardent advocate of the doctrines of the Reformers.

Others were present as eager listeners and attentive spectators; but upon these three young men, the sacred rite they witnessed for the first time produced permanent impressions that led to great results. The simplicity, the solemnity, the Scriptural beauty of the ordinance, touched their inmost hearts. The admonitions which accompanied it carried the truth with power to their souls. Henceforth these men will retain, through turbulent scenes, and amid the temptations of office, a faithful adherence to that Gospel which they have heard proclaimed at the table of the LORD's Supper in the hall of Calder-house.

Not without interest, then, shall we read these prayers and exhortations of the sacramental ser-

---

* HUME's *History of England*, ch. xl.

vice, whose first utterance three centuries ago fell on the ears of men with such power and force. We shall seem to hear, after their long silence, the tones of an earnest voice pronouncing these impressive words, which, it may be, have not utterly lost their efficacy to edify and instruct.*

THE MANNER OF THE ADMINISTRATION OF THE LORD'S SUPPER.

The day when the Lord's Supper is ministered, which is commonly used once a month, or so oft as the congregation shall think expedient, the minister useth to say as followeth.

Let us mark, dear brethren, and consider how JESUS CHRIST did ordain unto us his holy supper, according as St. Paul maketh rehearsal in the eleventh chapter of the First Epistle to the Corinthians, saying, I have received of the LORD that which also I delivered unto you, to wit, that the LORD JESUS, the same night in which he was betrayed, took bread, and when he had given thanks he brake it, and said, Take, eat; this is my body, which is broken for you: this do in

* DUNLOP'S *Coll. of Confessions, etc., of Public Authority in the Kirk of Scotland,* ii. 445.

remembrance of me. Likewise, after supper, he took the cup, saying, This cup is the new testament, or covenant, in my blood : this do, as oft as ye shall drink thereof, in remembrance of me. For as often as ye eat this bread, and drink of this cup, ye do show the LORD's death till he come. Wherefore whosoever shall eat this bread, and drink this cup of the LORD unworthily, he shall be guilty of the body and blood of the LORD. Then see that every one prove and try himself, and so let him eat of this bread and drink of this cup ; for he that eateth or drinketh unworthily, eateth and drinketh his own condemnation, for not having due regard and consideration of the LORD's body.

This done, the minister proceedeth to the exhortation.

Dearly beloved in the LORD, forasmuch as we be now assembled to celebrate the holy communion of the body and blood of our Saviour CHRIST, let us consider these words of St. Paul, how he exhorteth all persons diligently to try and examine themselves before they presume to eat of that bread, and to drink of that cup. For as the benefit is great, if with a true penitent heart and

lively faith we receive that holy sacrament (for
then we spiritually eat the flesh of CHRIST and
drink his blood, then we dwell in CHRIST, and
CHRIST in us, we be one with CHRIST and CHRIST
with us), so is the danger great if we receive the
same unworthily; for then we be guilty of the
body and blood of CHRIST our Saviour; we eat
and drink our own condemnation, not discerning
the LORD's body; we kindle GOD's wrath against
us, and provoke him to plague us with divers
diseases and sundry kinds of death.

And therefore, in the name and by the authority
of the eternal GOD, and of his Son JESUS CHRIST,
I excommunicate from this table all blasphemers
of GOD, all idolaters, all murderers, all adulterers,
all that be in malice or envy, all disobedient
persons to father or mother, to princes or magistrates, pastors or preachers, all thieves and de-
ceivers of their neighbours, and, finally, all such
as live a life directly fighting against the will of
GOD; charging them, as they will answer in the
presence of Him who is the righteous Judge, that
they presume not to profane this most holy table.
And yet this I pronounce not to seclude any
penitent person, how grievous soever his sins
before have been, so that he feel in his heart

unfeigned repentance for the same; but only such as continue in sin without repentance. Neither yet is this pronounced against such as aspire to a greater perfection than they can in this present life attain unto; for albeit we feel in ourselves much frailty and wretchedness, so that we have not our faith so perfect and constant as we ought, being many times ready to distrust GOD's goodness, through our corrupt nature; and also that we are not so thoroughly given to serve GOD, neither have so fervent a zeal to set forth his glory, as our duty requireth, feeling still such rebellion in ourselves, that we have need daily to fight against the lusts of our flesh; yet nevertheless, seeing that our LORD hath dealt thus mercifully with us, that he hath printed his Gospel in our hearts, so that we are preserved from falling into desperation and unbelief; and seeing also that he hath endued us with a will and desire to renounce and withstand our own affections, with a longing for his righteousness, and the keeping of his commandments: we may be now right well assured that those defaults and manifold imperfections in us shall be no hindrance at all against us, to cause Him not to accept and account us as worthy to come to his spiritual table. For the end of our coming thither is not to make protestation that we are upright or just in our lives, but contrariwise, we come to seek our life and perfection in JESUS CHRIST, acknowledging in the meantime that we of ourselves be the children of wrath and condemnation.

Let us consider, then, that this sacrament is a singular medicine for all poor sick creatures, a comfortable help to weak souls; and that our LORD requireth no other worthiness on our part, but that we unfeignedly acknowledge our sinfulness and imperfection. Then, to the end that we may be worthy partakers of his merits and most comfortable benefits (which is the true eating of his flesh and drinking of his blood), let us not suffer our minds to wander about the consideration of these earthly and corruptible things (which we see present to our eyes and feel with our hands), to seek CHRIST bodily present in them, as if he were inclosed in the bread and wine, or as if these elements were turned and changed into the substance of his flesh and blood. But as the only way to dispose our souls to receive nourishment, relief, and quickening of his substance, let us lift up our minds by faith above all things worldly and sensible, and thereby enter into heaven, that we may find and receive CHRIST, where he dwelleth undoubtedly, very GOD and very man, in the incomprehensible glory of his Father: To whom be all praise, honour, and glory, now and ever. Amen.

The exhortation ended, the minister cometh down from the pulpit, and sitteth at the table, every man and woman likewise taking their place as occasion best serveth: then he taketh bread, and giveth thanks, either in these words following, or like in effect:

O Father of Mercy, and GOD of all consolation! Seeing all creatures do acknowledge and confess thee as Governor and LORD: It becometh us, the workmanship of thine own hands, at all times to reverence and magnify thy godly Majesty. First, for that thou hast created us in thine own image and similitude: But chiefly in that thou hast delivered us from that everlasting death and damnation, into the which Satan drew mankind by the means of sin, from the bondage whereof neither man nor angel was able to make us free. We praise thee, O LORD! that thou, rich in mercy, and infinite in goodness, hast provided our redemption to stand in thine only and well-beloved Son, whom of very love thou didst give to be made man like unto us in all things, sin excepted, in his body to receive the punishment of our transgression, by his death to make satisfaction to thy justice, and through his resurrection to destroy him that was the author of death; and so to bring again life to the world, from which the whole offspring of Adam most justly was exiled.

O LORD! we acknowledge that no creature is able to comprehend the length and breadth, the depth and height of that thy most excellent love, which moved thee to show mercy where none was deserved, to promise and give life where death had gotten the victory, to receive us in thy grace when we could do nothing but rebel against thy justice. O LORD! the blind dulness of our corrupt nature will not suffer us sufficiently to weigh these thy most ample benefits; yet, nevertheless, at the commandment of JESUS CHRIST our Lord, we present ourselves at this His table, which he hath left to be used in remembrance of his death, until his coming again: to declare and witness before the world, that by him alone we have received liberty and life; that by him alone thou dost acknowledge us thy children and heirs; that by him alone we have entrance to the throne of thy grace; that by him alone we are possessed in our spiritual kingdom to eat and drink at his table, with whom we have our conversation presently in heaven, and by whom our bodies shall be raised up again from the dust, and shall be placed with him in that endless joy, which thou, O Father of Mercy! hast prepared for thine elect before the foundation of the world was laid. And these most inestimable benefits we acknowledge and confess to have received of thy free mercy and grace, by thine only beloved Son JESUS CHRIST: for the which, therefore, we thy congregation, moved by thine Holy Spirit, render all thanks, praise, and glory, for ever and ever. Amen.

This done, the minister breaketh the bread, and delivereth it to the people, who distribute and divide the same among themselves, according to our Saviour Christ's commandment, and likewise giveth the cup. During the which time some place of the Scriptures is read, which doth lively set forth the death of Christ, to the intent that our eyes and senses may not only be occupied in those outward signs of bread and wine, which are called the visible word, but that our hearts and mind also may be fully fixed in the contemplation of the Lord's death, which is by this holy sacrament represented; and after this action is done, he giveth thanks, saying:

Most merciful Father, we render to thee all praise, thanks, and glory, for that it hath pleased thee, of thy great mercies, to grant unto us, miserable sinners, so excellent a gift and treasure, as to receive us into the fellowship and company of thy dear Son JESUS CHRIST our Lord, whom thou hast delivered to death for us, and hast given him unto us as a necessary food and nourishment unto everlasting life. And now, we beseech thee also, O heavenly Father, to grant us this request, that thou never suffer us to become so unkind as to forget so worthy benefits; but rather imprint and fasten them sure in our hearts, that we may grow and increase daily more and more in true faith, which continually is exercised in all manner of good works; and so much the rather, O LORD, confirm us in these perilous days and rages of Satan, that we may constantly stand and continue in the confession of the same, to the advancement of thy glory, who art GOD over all things, blessed for ever. So be it. Amen.

The action thus ended, the people sing the hundred and third Psalm, or some other of thanksgiving; which ended, one of the blessings before mentioned is recited, and so they rise from the table, and depart.

VI.

Traces of the Scottish Liturgy.

"For my part I am apt to think,—that our prayers stood so long, was a favour by GOD granted us at the prayers of these men; who prayed *for* these prayers, as well as *in* them. And that they fell so soon, was a punishment of our negligence, who had not taught even those that liked them well, to use them aright."—ANON., 1650.

SUCH were the forms of worship introduced into the Church of Scotland at the Reformation, and observed with more or less uniformity* through the century succeeding. How general that observance, and how affected by subsequent legislation of the Church, let us proceed briefly to examine.

The Church of Scotland was represented at the Westminster Assembly (or "Synod of the Church of England," as it was then called) by commissioners appointed for that purpose. These deputies in 1645 reported the proceedings of the English

---

* *Absolute* uniformity was never intended. "There be two sorts of policy," says the First Book of Discipline (1560); "the one utterly necessary, as that the word be truly preached, the sacraments rightly ministered, common prayers publicly made, etc. The other is profitable merely, not necessary; as that psalms should be sung, that certain places of the Scriptures be read; that this day or that, or how many in the week, the Kirk should assemble; of these and such others we cannot see how a certain order can be established."—Ch. xi.

Synod, submitting to the General Assembly the
Confession of Faith, Book of Discipline, and
Directory of Worship which they had assisted in
framing. And in the same year, by act of General
Assembly, those formularies were "approved," and
adopted as standards of the Church of Scotland.*

The object of this legislation was clearly to fall
in with the action of the Westminster Divines, in
promoting uniformity among the churches, and
giving evidence of their perfect agreement. While
doing this, however, the Church made sacrifice of
her own peculiar standards;† those which had
been prepared for her by the earliest of the Reformers, and had continued in use until that day.
Along with her ancient Confession of Faith, Books
of Discipline, and Catechism, she gave up the
Book of Common Order, which had hitherto been
the directory of her worship.

* *Compendium of the Laws of the Church of Scotland*, Part Second,
p. 326.—Act Sess. 10, Feb. 3rd, 1645.

† This readiness to concede whatever might be necessary for union
and harmony, appears not to have been staggered by the unreason-
ableness of any demand. At the fourteenth Session of 1645, the
General Assembly resolved " that ministers bowing in the pulpit,
though a lawful custom in this Kirk, be thereafter laid aside, for the
satisfaction of the desires of the reverend divines in the Synod of
England, and for uniformity with that Kirk."—*Comp. of the Laws*,
etc., Part II. p. 327. This "bowing" to the people, at the commencement of the sermon, we have seen practised in some churches of
Saxony.

That this concession, made for the sake of unity, involved no *condemnation* of her former practice, the Church of Scotland took particular pains to declare. " It is also provided," says the decree by which conformity to the Westminster standards was enjoined, " that this act shall be no prejudice to the order and practice of this Kirk, in such particulars as are appointed by the *Books of Discipline* and acts of General Assemblies, and are not otherwise ordered and appointed by the Directory."* And another law forbids, under pain of ecclesiastical censure, " all condemning of one another, in such lawful things as had been *universally received, and by perpetual custom practised* by the most faithful ministers of the Gospel and opposers of corruptions in the Kirk, *since the first beginning of reformation to these times.*"†

It is evident from this language, that while the Church of Scotland consented to lay aside her proper and peculiar order of worship, with the hope of a general union of the British Churches in the newly proposed Directory of the Westminster Divines, she neither condemned nor abrogated that ancient formulary; but, on the

---

* *Compendium*, etc., Part II. p. 327.   Anno 1645.
† *Ibid.*, p. 326.   Anno 1643.

contrary, took special care to avoid the appearance of any such repudiation, by a distinct ratification of those acts and regulations, which had been passed in former Assemblies, approving the Book of Common Order.

We may now glance at the records of ecclesiastical action respecting the Order of Geneva, taken by the Church of Scotland on various occasions from the Reformation to the days of the Westminster Assembly.

In 1557, the year after its publication, the Order of Geneva was authorized, by the Lords of the Congregation, to be used in all churches.*

In 1560, the First General Assembly directed that " the Sacramentis suld be ministerit efter *the Order of the Kirk of Geneva*."† They mention it again as " the Book of our Common Order." They require that " a list of persons thought best qualified to preach, minister sacraments, and read the common prayers publickly in all kirks and congregations, be given in by ministers and commissioners."‡

In 1562, it was again confirmed by the General

---

* Bishop SAGE, " *The Fundamental Charter of Presbytery Examined*," p. 167.

† *First Book of Discipline*, ch. xi. DUNLOP'S *Confessions*, ii.

‡ *Compendium of Church Laws*, etc., Part II. p. 1.

Assembly, "that an uniform order should be kept in the ministration of the sacraments, solemnization of marriage, etc., according to the Kirk of Geneva."*

In 1564, a further act was passed, "ordaining, that every minister, exhorter, and reader, shall have one of the psalm-books lately printed in Edinburgh, and use the order therein contained, in prayers, marriage, and ministration of the sacraments, in the Book of Common Order."†
At another session of the same year, it was provided "that ministers have psalm-books, and use orders therein in prayers, marriage, and ministration of the sacraments."‡

In 1567, it was ordered, that the Book of Common Order, with Knox's prayers, be translated into Gaelic."§

In 1601, the General Assembly prohibited the making of any alterations or additions in the order of worship without submission of the proposed changes to itself; and nothing was thereafter added.‖

---

* Sage, "*Presbytery Examined,*" p. 167.
† *Comp. of Church Laws,* p. 14.
‡ *Ibid.,* p. 15.
§ Lorimer's *Prot. Churches of France and Scotland,* p. 144.
‖ " It being meinit be sundrie of the Brethren, that there was

After this date, we find no legislation on the subject. But that up to this period, and for the quarter of a century succeeding, the Book of Order was in common use, there is sufficient proof.

A Romish author writing in 1561, mentions it as the established form of prayers at that time.* When Queen Mary fled from Scotland to England, in 1568, " she feigned her willingness to give up with the mass, and to adopt the English Common Prayer-Book, provided Elizabeth would assist her in regaining her crown. Lord Herries having made this proposal in her name, Sir Francis Knollys, the English Ambassador, replied, ' that if he meant thereby to condemn the form and order of Common Prayer now used in Scotland, agreeable with divers well reformed churches: then he might so fight for the shadow and image of religion, that he might bring the body and truth into danger.' " †

---

sundrie Prayers in the Psalme Booke, quhilk wold be alterit, in respect they ar not convenient for the mean Tyme:—In the quhilk Head the Assembly has concludit, that it is not thocht good that the Prayeris alreadie conteinit in the Psalme Booke be alterit. But gif ony Brother wold have ony uther Prayers eikit quhilkis are meit for the Tyme, ordaynes the samen first to be tryit and allowit be the Assembly."—Dunlop's *Coll.*, ii. 513.

   * M'Crie's *Life of Knox, App.* p. 431.

   † *Ibid.*, p. 432.

When, in 1620, a Scottish clergyman was called before the High Commission, and accused of neglecting to minister the Eucharist to the people according to the Anglican forms, he answered: "There is no warrantable form directed or approven by the Kirk, besides that which is now extant in print before the Psalm Book; that is, the Old Liturgy; according to which, as I have always done, I now minister that sacrament."*

A writer of the seventeenth century states, that this form of worship continued to be used " even after the beginning of the horrid revolution (of 1648) in the days of King Charles I.; and many old people yet alive remember well" to have heard it read in the churches.†

Finally, in 1644, under the title of " The New Book of Scotland," an edition of the Order with some alterations was published, separate from the Psalm Book, to which hitherto it had been attached.‡

Thus we have shown, that as well by law as by

* CALDERWOOD, 748.—An edition of 1635, at Edinburgh, is mentioned by M'GAVIN, editor of *Knox's Hist. of the Reformation*, Glasgow, 1844.

† SAGE, *Presbytery Examined*, p. 351.

‡ JOHN KNOX'S LITURGY, an article in the Edinburgh Review, 1852.

custom, the form of worship introduced by John Knox continued to be the established and received Order of the Church of Scotland, until the period of her conformity with the standards of the Westminster Assembly.*

In England, also, the traces of this Liturgy, and of its frequent use, are to be met with along the latter part of the sixteenth century, and for some years later. And what is not a little remarkable, this use was not confined to those who sympathized with the Christians of Scotland in their opposition to prelacy and the English ritual. We find the prayers of Knox's Liturgy adopted even in the Church of England, for purposes of private devotion.†

Knox and his colleagues at Geneva, when they first published the Order of Worship drawn up for the English congregation of that city, dedicated it to their brethren in England;‡ and the proba-

* The latest publication of this formulary was in 1840, when it appeared at London, in a small volume edited, with a short preface, by the distinguished Scottish minister, Dr. Cumming. His strongly recommendatory notices of these forms we shall have occasion to refer to again. Prefixed to the Psalm-book now in use at the Scottish National Church in London, is a portion of Knox's Liturgy.

† *Private Prayers published during the reign of Queen Elizabeth.* Parker Society, 1851.

‡ *Preface to the Book of Common Order.* DUNLOP'S *Confessions,* ii. 385.

bility seems strong, that it came into immediate and extensive use among the Protestants of that kingdom who refused or hesitated to conform with the Established Church. Both in London and on the Continent there were printed at this period a multitude of editions of the Psalms and Prayers used in Scotland.*

During the reign of Mary, there was a congregation formed at London by the Protestants, who met in secret, for fear of persecution, to celebrate Divine worship according to the Scottish forms.† In the time of Elizabeth we find similar conventicles, where the same rites were observed.‡ And it is natural to infer, that all the congregations of Dissenters or Separatists existing at that period, were in the habit of using these services, which had been adopted by the Churches of Geneva and Scotland, to whose doctrine and discipline they were strongly attached.§

In the years 1584 and 1586, attempts were made in Parliament to obtain sanction for " the

* LORIMER's *Protestant Church of France*, p. 144.

† GRINDAL's *Remains*, p. 204.

‡ STRYPE's *Whitgift*, iii. 278. GRINDAL's *Remains*, p. 204.

§ At an examination of Nonconformist preachers during the reign of Elizabeth, 1588-9, no fewer than nine ministers are named as having been guilty of performing worship according to the " Form used at Geneva."—STRYPE's *Whitgift*, iii. 278.

Form of Prayers and Administration of the Sacraments used in the English Church at Geneva; approved and received by the Church of Scotland."[*]   Though the attempt was unsuccessful, it became customary to publish the substance of these prayers in connexion with the Liturgy of the Church of England, appended to the authorized editions of the Sacred Scriptures; and they are to be found so printed in various editions of the Bible, from the year 1590 to the year 1640. It was evidently designed that these forms should be used in secret or social worship only; indeed, they are headed with the title: "A Forme of Prayer to be used in private houses every Morning and Evening." But a comparison of these prayers with those of Knox's Liturgy will prove them to be identical.

Such are the traces of the existence and use of the Scottish Liturgy, down to the middle of the seventeenth century. Until supplanted by the Directory of Worship, it remained the chosen and

* HOOKER'S *Works*, ii. 159, *note*. STRYPE'S *Whitgift*, i. 347, 487. "A new platform of ecclesiastical government, agreeable to that of Geneva, and another form of Common Prayer prescribed therein, in the room of the old one, for this Church."—In Parliament, 27 Elizabeth. The title of this book is given thus by Strype: "The Sacred Discipline of the Church described in the Word of GOD, 1584."

voluntary formulary of the Calvinistic party in England, as well as the prescribed order of the Church of Scotland. But after the period of the Westminster Assembly, we find no mention of it, nor is there reason to doubt that it then fell into complete disuse.

VIII.

Worship of the Early Puritans.

"Juxta laudabilem Ecclesiæ Scotiæ Reformatæ formam et ritum."
ARCHBISHOP GRINDAL, 1582.

On a Sunday morning, in the month of June, 1567, some peaceable citizens of London were gathered to the number of about one hundred, in a hall engaged for the purpose, to worship GOD after the dictates of their conscience. Most of them evidently belonged to the class of trades-people and mechanics; but a few might be recognised as ministers of the Gospel; being such as the recent laws of conformity had ejected from their livings and forbidden to preach. Their present meeting was in disregard of an unjust enactment prohibiting all religious assemblies elsewhere than in consecrated buildings. As each worshipper entered the room, he stood for a moment reverently with bowed head in silent prayer; till at length one of them, dressed in the peculiar garb of the Calvinistic preachers, advancing to the Communion-table, began the services of the occasion; and stretching forth his hands, solemnly uttered the invocation of the Psalmist:

"Our help is in the Name of the LORD, who made heaven and earth. Amen."

These words were appropriate for the opening of an act of worship, and in fact belonged to the ritual of the Reformed service. But they had a timely meaning for those poor "Londoners" thus congregated in secrecy, and now just about to be seized and cast into prison for conscience' sake and the Gospel's. Well for them if they could of a truth put their hope of help in that high Name of the LORD who made heaven and earth; for they were to find little mercy and forbearance at the hands of men calling themselves his servants.

It was under the reign of Elizabeth that the incidents we are relating occurred; but nineteen years after the formal establishment of the Protestant religion in the realm. The poor Calvinists who were thus meeting in private for their religious rites,* were most of them among the original

* "These latter separated themselves into private assemblies, meeting together, not in churches, but in private houses, where they had ministers of their own. And at these meetings, rejecting wholly the Book of Common Prayer, they used a book of prayers framed at Geneva for the congregation of English exiles lately sojourning there.

converts from Popery and receivers of the doctrine
of the Reformers. In fact, they had heard the
pure faith preached by the earliest of its advocates,
and perhaps witnessed the good profession of many
who perished as martyrs in the bloody reign of
Mary. Not much wonder if such men preferred
the simple form of worship which they adopted
when relinquishing Romish superstition, to rites
and ceremonies savouring, to their plain taste, of
the old pernicious leaven.

Such was their occupation, when this little
assembly was disturbed by an unexpected intru-
sion. Several sheriffs, hastily entering the room,
broke up the meeting, and arrested some fourteen or fifteen among them, who were ministers
of the Gospel, dispersing the rest, while their
companions were carried off to prison. There
they lay until sent for the next day to appear
before " the Lord Mayor, the Bishop of London,
and others the Queen's Commissioners," on charge
of disobedience to the laws of the realm. Their examination before these worshipful authorities must
have presented a singular spectacle. Here were

Which book had been overseen and allowed by Calvin, and the rest
of his divines there; and indeed was for the most part taken out of
the Geneva form."—STRYPE's *Life of Arch. Grindal*, b. i., c. 10.

men of good character and favourable appearance summoned on no charge of crime save that of peacefully assembling in Christian worship; and this before a Protestant prelate who, as we shall see, in former days of persecution, had himself taken part in the very same rites of worship, similarly performed in a foreign city to which he had retreated. We have had the good fortune to come across a full account of this extraordinary trial, as written down from the lips of the men themselves; it is contained in a rare pamphlet entitled, " The Examination of certain Londoners before the Ecclesiastical Commissioners, June 20th, 1567."

The colloquy between these honest and brave-hearted men, and the well-meaning, though vacillating Grindal, then Bishop of London, is as quaint and striking as that recorded by Bunyan between Faithful and his judges in Vanity Fair. Here is the main part of it, in their own old-fashioned words : *—

" When we were come in," say the Londoners, " we did our obeisance, and they bade us come near, and the Bishop's registrar called us by

* " *The Examination of certain Londoners,*" etc., in GRINDAL'S *Life and Remains.* London : Parker Society.

name; John Smith, William Nixson, William White, James Ireland, Robert Hawkins, Thomas Boweland, and Richard Morecroft. The Bishop said, Is here all? One answered, No, there are ten or eleven in the Compter.

Bishop. I know that well enough.

The Bishop said unto the Mayor, My Lord, will you begin? The Mayor said unto him, I pray you begin.

Bishop. Well, then, here you have showed yourselves disorderly, not only in absenting yourselves from your parish churches, and the assemblies of other Christians in this commonwealth, which do quietly obey the Queen's proceedings, and serve GOD in such good order as the Queen's grace and the rest having authority and wisdom have set forth and established by Act of Parliament: but, also, ye have gathered together and made assemblies, using prayers and preachings, yea, and ministering the sacraments among yourselves. And thus, you gather together many times; yea, and no longer ago than yesterday you were together to the number of an hundred; whereof there were about fourteen or fifteen of you sent to prison. And our being here is to will you to leave off, or else you shall see the Queen's letter, and the Council's hands at it. (Then he opened it, and showed it us, but would not read it. The effect of it, he said, was to move us to be conformable by gentleness, or else at the first we should lose our freedom of the city, and abide that would follow.) * * * In this severing yourselves from the society of other Christians, you condemn not only us, but also the whole state of the Church reformed in King Edward's days, which was well reformed according to the word of GOD, yea, and many good men have shed their blood for the same, which your doings condemn.

Hawkins. We condemn them not, in that we stand to the truth of GOD's word.

But he would not suffer us to answer to it.

Bishop. But have you not the Gospel truly preached, and the sacraments ministered accordingly, and good order kept, although we differ from other churches in ceremonies, and in indifferent things, which lie in the prince's power to command for order's sake? How say you, Smith? You seem to be the ancientest of them; answer you.

Smith. Indeed, my Lord, we thank GOD for reformation; and that is it we desire, according to GOD's word.   (And there he stayed.)

White. I beseech you, let me answer.

Bishop. Nay, William White, hold your peace; you shall be heard anon.

Nixson. I beseech you, let me answer a word or two.

Bishop. Nixson, you are a busy fellow, I know your words; you are full of talk; I know from whence you came.

Hawkins. I would be glad to answer.

Bishop. Smith shall answer. Answer you, Smith.

Smith. Indeed, as you said even now, for preaching and ministering the sacraments, so long as we might have the word freely preached, and the sacraments administered without the preferring of idolatrous gear about it, we never assembled together in houses. But when it came to this point, that all our preachers were displaced by your law, that would not subscribe to your apparel and your law, so that we could not hear none of them in any church by the space of seven or eight weeks, except Father Coverdale, of whom we have a good opinion, (and yet, GOD knoweth, the man was so fearful, that he durst not be known unto us where he preached, though we sought it at his house : then we bethought us what were best to

do.   And we remembered that there was a congregation of us in this city in Queen Mary's days ;
and a congregation at Geneva, which used a book
and order of preaching, ministering of the sacraments and discipline, most agreeable to the word
of GOD ; which book is allowed by that godly and
well-learned man, Master Calvin, and the preachers
there ; which book and order we now hold.   And
if you can reprove this book, or anything that we
hold, by the word of GOD, we will yield to you,
and do open penance at Paul's Cross ; if not, we
will stand to it by the grace of GOD.

Bishop. This is no answer.

White. You may be answered, if you will give
leave.   * * *   I delivered a book to Justice
Harris, which is the order that we hold.   Reprove
the same by the word of GOD, and we will leave
it and give over.

Bishop. We cannot reprove it.   But to gather
together disorderly, to trouble the common quiet
of the realm against the prince's will, we like not
the holding of it.

Hawkins. Why, that which we do, we do it
by the commandment of GOD ; we have the
example of the first and apostolic Church for our
warrant, as in the 16th to the Romans, ver. 17.

" I beseech you, brethren, mark them that cause divisions, and give occasions of evil, contrary to the doctrine which ye have learned, and avoid them."

Dean. Yea, but the manner which ye hold is unorderly, and against the authority of the prince.

Hawkins. Why, the truth of God is a truth, wheresoever it be holden, or whosoever doth hold it ; except ye will make it subject to places and persons, and to the authority of the prince. It had been better we had never been born, than to suffer GOD to be dishonoured, and his word defaced for princes' pleasures.

Bishop. All the learned are against you ; will you be tried by them ?

White. We will be tried by the word of GOD ; which shall judge us all at the last day. * * * We will be tried by the best Reformed Churches. The Church of Scotland hath the word truly preached, the sacraments truly ministered, and discipline according to the word of GOD ; and these be the notes by which the true Church is known."

So, after some further discussion, ended this curious examination : to the end of which the reporter adds these words : " From hence to prison

they went, all or most of them. Such was the
great charity of the bishops! And till their day
of deliverance they never knew one good word
they spoke for them, though divers of them had
wives and children, and were but poor men."

A whole year these innocent Christian people
lay in prison! and that under the Protestant
reign of "that bright Occidental Star, Queen
Elizabeth of most happy memory." Alas, for the
rarity of Christian charity! Out of their doleful
bondage they could utter no voice of remonstrance ;
but at length, with tardy compassion, the bishop
obtained an order for their release : and they
were discharged, to the number of twenty-four men,
besides seven women !

When these sufferers and their brethren made
some complaint of this treatment, in a supplication
to the Privy Council for relief from the hindrances
to which they were subjected, they seem to have
been considered rather unreasonable ! Here is the
tenor of their petition :

" We beseech your honours, for GOD's cause,
favourably to consider of these few lines. The
effect is to certify you, that whereas a certain of
us poor men of the city were kept in prison one
whole year for our conscience' sake, because we

would serve our GOD by the rule of his holy word, without the vain and wicked ceremonies and traditions of papistry; and being delivered forth the 23rd of April last past, by authority of the honourable Council's letter, as the bishop declared to us all at his house, the third of May, saying, that means had been made to your honours for our liberty; the effect thereof, he said, was, that we were freed from our parish churches, and that we might hear such preachers that we liked best of in the city: also, whereas we requested to have baptism truly ministered to our children according to the word and order of the Geneva book : he said that he would tolerate it, and appoint two or three to do it ; immediately after, at our request, he appointed two preachers, called Bonham and Crane, under his handwriting, to keep a lecture.

" But now of late, because Bonham did marry a couple, and baptize one of our children, by the order of the said book, which is most sincere, he hath commanded him to be kept close prisoner ; and Mr. Crane also he hath commanded not to preach in his diocese.

" By these means were we driven at first to forsake the churches, and to congregate in our houses. Now we protest to your honour, we never yielded to no condition in our coming forth of prison, but minded to stand fast in the same sincerity of the Gospel that we did when we were in prison, approved and commanded of GOD in his word. And therefore we humbly beseech your honours to let us have your furtherance and help in so good a cause : that our bodies and goods be no more molested for standing in this good purpose which we most heartily desire to see flourish throughout this realm, to GOD's high honour, the preservation of your honourable personages, and safeguard of this realm."

No redress followed upon this humble remonstrance, which indeed seems to have been designed rather to vindicate the consistency of the petitioners, than to obtain redress. There is the ring of true metal about these words, which would have done credit to old martyrs and confessors : " Now we protest to your honours, WE NEVER YIELDED TO NO CONDITION in our coming forth of prison, but minded to stand fast in the same sincerity of the Gospel that we did when we were in prison, approved and commanded of GOD in his word."

We hasten to point out the bearing of these facts respecting the early Puritans, upon the subject of our present researches. It is apparent from their own statements here quoted, that these sufferers for the Gospel, in their first humble and secret assemblies, forbidden by law and exposed to sudden disturbance, followed the order and manner of the Scottish and Genevan ritual. The fathers of Nonconformity in England were no advocates of loose and irregular practises in the celebration of religious rites. They discarded the offensive Liturgy of the prelates, not to abandon all forms, but to substitute a pure, simple, and evangelical form, which had been established and approved by all the " best reformed churches."

And there is reason to believe that this adoption of the Calvinistic mode of worship, was universal among the first congregations of the Nonconformists. In the preceding chapter we have seen, that many, if not all, of those preachers who, under the reign of Elizabeth, were tried and punished for the crime of separation from the Established Church, had been in the habit of performing worship according to the " Form used at Geneva." It was not until a much later day, that this invaluable Liturgy began to fall into neglect; and that doubtless owing rather to the disorders of the times, than to any change of sentiment regarding the proper celebration of Divine worship.   Even as we shall hereafter see, in the days of Calamy and Baxter, that prejudice against ritual services which is commonly imputed to the Puritans, had not yet spread throughout their body.

While we honour and admire the earnest piety and firm principle of these excellent men whose trials we have here depicted, it must be conceded that in some respects their views were narrowed by strong and unreasonable antipathies. There was already manifest a disposition to oppose and condemn innocent and even commendable practices belonging to that system of worship from which they dissented. Thus among certain articles or statements of errors requiring redress, in the Anglican Church, drawn up by some of the early Nonconformists, we find the following:—

"No sacrament ought to be administered without being preceded by a sermon, *preached and not read.*

"Sermons ought not to be preached at the burial of the dead.

"The Holy Scriptures ought not to be read in the churches.

"No one ought to be confined to set forms of prayer."*

* ZURICH LETTERS, p. 417.

The last of these requirements, though perfectly compatible with the free use of a Liturgy, was severely condemned by the learned theologian Gualter, minister at Zurich in Switzerland ; who, on being informed of the opinions advanced by these preachers, wrote in the following terms :—

"Where they say that no one ought to be tied down to set forms of prayer, I know not in what sense they make the assertion. If they mean this, that we are not superstitiously to attach any virtue to preconceived words of prayer, or to certain forms of prayer, I am also of the same opinion; for this rather belongs to exorcists and conjurors. But if they condemn certain forms of public prayer, I should say that they are mad with their wits about them. * * * For that such prayers have been in use in all ages, no one can deny ; and it is more than necessary that they should be retained. * * * But yet this does not prevent individuals from offering their prayers in private for themselves. * * * And ministers also may subjoin, at the close of their sermons, prayers suitable to the subject of which they have been treating."*

But here we leave the persecuted Nonconformists of the days of Queen Elizabeth, and turn to look

* ZURICH LETTERS, p. 446.

at their Episcopal opponent, before whose tribunal they found so little compassion for their weaknesses, and toleration of their conscientious persuasions.

Poor Bishop Grindal! it was hard for so well-meaning and truly pious a man as he certainly was, to be thus placed in the position of a relentless persecutor of the faithful. He could find no fault with their doctrines, which were as thoroughly orthodox as his own. Nay, he had nothing to impugn in their book of worship, as he avows when they offer to defend it: "We cannot reprove it." Moreover, as intimated already, the good bishop could not but remember that only some thirteen years before, he had taken part in these very rites which he was now condemning; when uniting at Strasburg and Frankfort, with other English exiles, in celebrating religious worship.*

But another feature of the case deserves to be noted. In 1563, only four years earlier than the period on which we have been dwelling, the Plague broke out in England, and soon extending to London, committed great ravages there. Grindal

* See STRYPE's *Life of Grindal.* The archbishop entertained the highest veneration for the Churches and pastors of Geneva in his day. He calls that city, " A nursery unto GOD."—B. ii., c. 14.

was called upon to draw up a Form of Prayer and Fasting suitable to the time of this severe visitation. And in performing this duty, what does the worthy bishop do, but go to the old Order of Geneva, the Calvinistic Liturgy which he had seen used at Frankfort, and which he afterwards condemned the use of in his own diocese of London; and from that he takes, whole and entire, the beautiful prayer there appointed for an exigency against which his own Book of Common Prayer contained no provision!* Surely these recollections must have sorely troubled the good man's conscience when sitting in judgment upon the unfortunate "Londoners" guilty of using that Order of Geneva, which he himself had "used" to such good purpose on so memorable an occasion. Perhaps to this reminiscence the poor defendants owed his concession : "We cannot reprove it."†

All this leads us to look with some interest upon the Form of Prayer in question. The original,

* He was required to do this work in great haste (see STRYPE, b. i., c. 7); which may somewhat account for the plagiarism.

† "In the year 1582, Archbishop Grindal, by a formal deed, declared the validity of the orders of Mr. John Morrison, who had been ordained by the Synod of Lothian, according to the laudable form and rite of the Reformed Church of Scotland. Says the instrument : 'Per generalem synodum sive congregationem illius comitatus, juxta laudabilem ecclesiæ Scotiæ Reformatæ formam

composed by Calvin, will be found in his Works.[*] Grindal's translation we give in the main as follows :[†] premising that the prayer thus credited to the bishop was the basis upon which other forms of prayer, in times of public danger, were afterwards drawn up during the Queen's reign :—

O ALMIGHTY, most just and merciful GOD! we acknowledge ourselves unworthy to lift up our eyes unto heaven, as we present ourselves before thee. For our consciences accuse us, and our sins reprove us; and we know that thou who art a righteous Judge, must needs punish them that transgress thy law. O LORD! when we look back and examine our whole life, we find nothing in ourselves that deserveth any other reward than eternal condemnation. But since thou, of thine unspeakable mercy, hast commanded us in all our necessities to call upon thee; and hast also

---

et ritum, ad sacros ordines et sacrosanctum ministerium per manuum impositionem admissus et ordinatus. Nos igitur formam ordinationis et præfectionis tuæ hujus modi, modo præmisso factam, quantum in nos est, et de jure possumus, approbantes et ratificantes,'" etc.—STRYPE'S *Life of Grindal*, quoted in M'CRIE'S *Life of John Knox*, p. 49, *note*.

[*] OPUSCULA, Liturgy of the Church- of Geneva. Compare *A Godly Prayer*, in the Book of Common Order; DUNLOP'S *Confessions*, ii. 481. Also, *A Prayer on the Lord's Day after Sermon*, in the Reformed Dutch Liturgy. And *A Prayer for the Queen's Majesty*, in the "Private Prayers" of the Parker Society, p. 447.

[†] Conforming in some few passages more closely to the original.

promised that thou wilt hear our prayers, not for any merit of our own, for we have none, but for the merits of thy Son, whom thou hast ordained to be our only Mediator and Intercessor: Therefore, we lay aside all confidence in man, and flee to the throne of thy mercy, by the intercession of thy only Son our Saviour, JESUS CHRIST.

O LORD! we do lament and bewail, from the bottom of our hearts, our past unthankfulness towards thee. We remember that besides those benefits of thine which we enjoy in common with all men as thy creatures, thou hast bestowed upon us many special blessings, of which we are not able in heart to conceive the value, much less in words worthily to express it. Thou hast called us to the knowledge of thy Gospel. Thou hast released us from the hard servitude of Satan. Thou hast delivered us from all idolatry, wherein we were sunken; and hast brought us into the clear and comfortable light of thy blessed word. But we, most unmindful in our prosperity of these thy great benefits, have neglected thy commandments, have abused the knowledge of thy Gospel, have followed our carnal liberty, have served our own lusts, and through our sinful lives have failed suitably to serve and honour thee.

And now, O LORD! compelled by thy correction, we do most humbly confess that we have sinned, and have most grievously displeased thee. And if thou, O LORD! provoked with our disobedience, shouldst now deal with us as we have deserved, there remaineth nothing to be looked for, but continual plagues in this world, and hereafter eternal death and condemnation, both of body and of soul. For if we should excuse ourselves, our own consciences would accuse us before thee, and our own disobedience and wickedness would bear witness against us. Yea, even thy plagues and punishments, which thou dost now lay upon us in sundry places, teach us to acknowledge our sins. For seeing that thou art just, O LORD! yea, even justice itself, thou dost not punish any without desert. And now, O LORD! we see thy hand terribly stretched out to plague us, and punish us.*
Yet, although thou shouldst punish us more grievously still; though thou shouldst pour upon us all those testimonies of thy just wrath, which in time past thou pouredst on thy chosen people Israel; yet could we not deny that we had justly deserved it.

---

* This prayer was written by Calvin for the Church of Geneva in 1541, "when Germany was infested both with war and pestilence." "Precationes, quibus in iis uterentur, conscripsi." — *Calv. Ep.*, quoted by BINGHAM, *Works*, ii. 748.

But, O merciful LORD! thou art our GOD, and we are thine inheritance; thou art our Creator, and we the work of thy hands; thou art our Pastor, we are thy flock; thou art our Redeemer, and we the people whom thou hast redeemed; thou art our Father, we are thy children. LORD! be not wroth against us; punish us not in thy sore displeasure.

Remember, O LORD! that thy name hath been named upon us; that we bear thy seal and the tokens of thy service. Perfect the work thou hast begun in us; that all the world may know thou art our GOD and merciful Deliverer. Thou knowest that the dead who are in their graves cannot praise thee; but the sorrowful spirit, the contrite heart, the conscience broken with a sense of sin, and panting for thy grace, shall give thee praise and glory. Thy people Israel ofttimes offended thee, and thou didst justly afflict them; but as oft as they returned to thee, thou didst receive them in mercy; and though their sins were never so great, yet didst thou turn away thy wrath, and the punishment prepared for them; and that for thy covenant's sake, which thou madest with thy servants Abraham, Isaac, and Jacob. Thou hast made a better covenant with us, O heavenly

Father! a covenant on which we may lean as we appear before thee: through the mediation of thy dear Son JESUS CHRIST our Saviour, with whose most precious blood it pleased thee that this covenant should be written, sealed, and confirmed.

Wherefore, O heavenly Father! we now, casting away all confidence in ourselves or any other creature, do flee to this most holy covenant and testament; wherein our Lord and Saviour JESUS CHRIST, once offering himself a sacrifice for us on the cross, hath reconciled us to thee for ever. Look, therefore, O merciful GOD! not upon the sins which we continually commit, but upon our Mediator and Peacemaker, JESUS CHRIST: that by his intercession thy wrath may be pacified, and we again by thy fatherly countenance relieved and comforted. Receive us also into thy heavenly defence, and govern us by thy Holy Spirit. Frame in us newness of life, wherein to laud and magnify thy blessed name for ever, and to live every one of us according to the several states of life whereunto thou hast ordained us.

And, O heavenly Father! although, by reason of our past sins, we are unworthy to crave anything of thee: yet because thou hast commanded us to pray for all men, we most humbly beseech thee,

M

save and defend thy holy Church. Be merciful
to all commonwealths, countries, princes, and
magistrates; and especially to this our realm,
and to our most gracious governor, Queen Elizabeth. Increase the number of godly ministers.
Endue them with thy grace, to be found faithful
and prudent in their office. Defend the Council
of the Queen's majesty, and all that be in
authority under her, or that serve in any place by
her commandment. We commend also to thy
fatherly mercy all that be in poverty, exile,
imprisonment, sickness, or any other kind of
adversity; and chiefly those whom thy hand hath
now touched with any contagious and dangerous
sickness; which we beseech thee, O LORD! of thy
mercy, when thy blessed will is, to remove. And
in the meantime grant grace and true repentance,
steadfast faith, and constant patience: that
whether we live or die, we may always continue
thine, and ever bless thy holy name, and be
brought to the fruition of thy Godhead. Grant
these, and all our humble petitions, O merciful
Father! for the sake of thy dear Son JESUS CHRIST
our Lord. Amen.

IX.

Baxter's Reformed Liturgy.

"We are satisfied in our judgments concerning the lawfulness of a liturgy, or form of public worship; provided that it be for the matter agreeable unto the Word of GOD, and fitly suited to the nature of the several ordinances and necessities of the Church."

FIRST ADDRESS OF THE MINISTERS.

THE Conference which took place at the Savoy in 1660, between twelve leaders of the Nonconformist party and an equal number of prelates of the Church of England, was the last ostensible effort to reconcile their differences, and bring about a formal agreement. But in reality, as we review the transactions of that meeting, it is easy to perceive that on neither side did there exist an intention to reach by compromise and concession these desirable ends. The scheme of reconciliation was a political device, and failed to receive the cordial co-operation of either of the conflicting parties. The bishops stood upon their dignity, determined to yield nothing, while the Puritans were as rigid in their demands. The former aimed only at an apparent compliance with the royal requisition, while evading even the most trivial alteration of existing institutions. The latter, hopeless of realizing their proposed amendments, were chiefly anxious for an "opportunity of leaving upon record their testimony against corruptions," and their desires for "a just and moderate reformation" of abuses.

Accordingly, Baxter and his colleagues, who represented the Nonconformist interests at the Savoy Conference, brought in a list of exceptions to the Prayer Book, many of which were reasonable, and ought to have been readily granted, while others were certainly impracticable or uncalled for. The unbending temper of the bishops made no discrimination between these classes of objections, and their treatment of them was calculated to awaken a corresponding disposition in their opponents.

No hope of emendation in the Prayer Book could long be entertained by the Puritan divines who assembled at the conference of the Savoy. Indeed, "where undistinguishing admiration is directed to works of merely human composition, it cannot be expected that any alterations will be regarded otherwise than in the light of captious and unnecessary innovations."* The chief object

* ORME'S *Life and Times of Baxter*, p. 220.

of the Nonconformists then became, to obtain the liberty of using among themselves such forms of worship as they could agree upon, leaving the Prayer Book to stand as it was. In other words, they desired the adoption of a Reformed Liturgy in addition to that ritual already in use, in order that those who could not conscientiously receive the one might adopt the other.

We cannot see that this proposition deserved the ridicule with which it was regarded by the prelatical party. If the winning over of so large and respectable a body of men as that headed by Baxter and Calamy, was an object worthy of the least sacrifice, these men did not ask too much in proposing such an enlargement of the mode of worship as would comprehend their usages and views. The party existed, and claimed consideration for its numbers and influence. It comprised multitudes of the most sincere and correct professors of Christianity in the realm, with not a few individuals of distinguished name. We may question, therefore, whether a liberal and enlightened policy, to say nothing of a higher wisdom, should not have acceded to a project which, without compromising the doctrines and order of the Establishment, was calculated to draw into it so large a body of Christians. Such a course was not without precedent in the history of religion. Rome has suffered to remain for centuries more than one ritual which she has found in use among the churches over which her sway has extended.* She allows at the present day no inconsiderable variations from her own formularies, even in the order of the Mass.† The saints and the festivals of each national rite, with their appropriate offices of devotion, have been incorporated into her Liturgy; while the wisdom of such a course is made evident by the fact, that the Roman rite gradually predominating, has in most cases, after a time, replaced the provincial peculiarities of worship. Nor was the alleged frivolity of the Puritan objections to the Prayer Book a valid reason for rejecting their demand. If these exceptions were so unimportant, doubtless a moderate and conciliatory treatment would in time have softened prejudice and induced conformity. But, unfortunately, alike for the Estab-

---

* "Debet unaquæque ecclesia custodire ritus suos, sed receptos a majoribus, longoque usu præscriptos, et legitima auctoritate approbatos."—BONA, *Ref. Lit.*, lib. vi.

† In the Ambrosian and Gallican rites more particularly: for the former of which consult " *Il modo di servire la Santa Messa, secondo il Rito Ambrosiano e Romano.*" Milan, 1849.

lishment and the Dissenters, no such spirit reigned in the councils of the Savoy.

The Puritans have been the objects of further obloquy in consequence of a misapprehension of their demands. It has been said that they required the abolishment of the Prayer Book, and the substitution of a hastily-prepared ritual of their own. The impracticable nature of such a request would reduce the transactions of the Savoy to a mere farce, or a designed mockery. But this statement is incorrect. Baxter, in his address introducing the proposed Nonconformist Liturgy, prays that it may be adopted as well as the old, and that either of them be used, at the discretion of the minister.* The great purpose for which he and his brethren had sought the appointment of such a Conference, was to obtain " an addition or insertion of some other varying forms in Scripture phrase, to be used at the minister's choice."† This object the royal declaration convoking the assembly of the Savoy clearly ratifies and approves. It commands the preparation of " some *additional forms*, in the Scripture phrase as near as may be, suited unto the nature of the several parts of

* CARDWELL, *Conferences on the Book of Common Prayer*, p. 261.
† *First Address of the Ministers*, in CARDWELL, p. 282.

worship, and that *it be left to the minister's choice*
to use one or other at his discretion."* Nothing
more than this did the Puritan divines attempt;
but the bishops refused utterly to entertain the
proposal. †

On the general subject of Liturgies, the senti-

* *King Charles's Declaration*, etc. In CARDWELL, pp. 294, 295.
† "That which hath been is now." In our own day the wisdom
of this proposal, made by Baxter and his colleagues, and spurned by
the entire bench of the prelates, is receiving confirmation where
least expected. A scheme of improvement in the worship and discipline of the Protestant Episcopal Church in the United States, has
for some months past engaged the attention of the bishops of that
Church. We cannot pause to specify the reforms advocated by the
'Memorial of sundry Presbyters," which was presented to that body,
and which forms the subject of their deliberations. But in an
"Exposition" of that memorial, prepared by a clergyman of high
character and standing, who is regarded as the principal author of
this movement, a remarkable feature is to be observed. The identical
privilege sought by Baxter and his brethren,—that of discretionary variation and substitution in the use of the Liturgy,—is here
demanded by an eminent minister of the Episcopal Church. Nay,
the very improvement solicited then,—the addition of "some forms
in the Scripture phrase as near as may be, to be used at the
minister's choice,"—is here suggested, almost in the same language.
"Let there be an *Appendix*," urges the distinguished author of the
Exposition, "for the benefit of those who might choose to use it;
containing * * * Scripture hymns and anthems, *prayers* * * * *which
also might be very much in Scripture words.*" Surely, the justice
and propriety of those demands, which were so contemptuously
slighted by the prelates of Baxter's day, could not be more strikingly
vindicated than by such a resuscitation. All honour to the candid,
enlightened, and truly Christian spirit which inspired this movement in the mind of its excellent projector. If such counsels could
have reigned at the Savoy two centuries ago, what dissensions and
controversies would not have been spared the Church of CHRIST!

ment of the Nonconformist ministers is fully represented in their letter to the king. "We are satisfied in our judgments," say they, "concerning the lawfulness of a liturgy, or form of public worship; provided that it be for the matter agreeable to the Word of GOD, and fitly suited to the nature of the several ordinances and institutions of the Church; neither too tedious in the whole, nor composed of too short prayers, unmeet repetitions or responsals; not to be dissonant from the liturgies of other reformed Churches; nor too rigorously imposed; nor the minister so confined thereunto, but that he may also make use of those gifts for prayer and exhortation which CHRIST hath given him for the service and edification of the Church."*

The task of preparing such a formulary of worship as would meet the wishes and wants of the Nonconformist churches, was unanimously assigned by his colleagues to Richard Baxter. He was a man of pre-eminent and acknowledged qualifications for the work. His devotional writings had been numerous, and most acceptable to the churches. His gifts for the conception and utterance of the language of prayer were remark-

* *First Address*, etc. In CARDWELL, p. 282.

able even in an age when such endowments were
cultivated to a very high degree. " His prayers,"
says a contemporary, " were an effusion of the
most lively, melting expressions of his intimate,
ardent affections to GOD : from the abundance of
the heart his lips spake. His soul took wing for
heaven, and rapt up the souls of others with him.
Never did I see or hear a holy minister address
himself to GOD with more reverence or humility,
with respect to his glorious greatness : never with
more zeal and fervency, correspondent to the
infinite number of his requests, nor with more
filial affiance in the Divine mercy."*

It required, indeed, this great facility of devotional composition, if we may so speak, to enable
Baxter, in the short space of a *fortnight,* to
prepare a Liturgy of such amplitude and excellence. In the haste of the convocation, no longer
time was allowed him; "nor could he make use
of any book, except a Bible and a Concordance ;
but he compared it all with the Assembly's
Directory, and the Book of Common Prayer."
Whatever traces of this imperfect execution the
work may have borne, however, do not appear to

* Dr. BATES, quoted in ORME's *Life and Times of Baxter,* p. 407.

have come to the notice of the bishops; for they never bestowed the trouble of a glance at its contents, when submitted to their inspection. As subsequently given to publication, it underwent considerable improvement by the careful revision of the author; and certainly shows little evidence of haste in its present condition. "Without pronouncing on the comparative excellencies of this liturgical work, or intimating that it is everything that such a work should be, it is not too much to say, that it is remarkable for simplicity, appropriateness, and fulness. The forms of prayer contain variety without repetition, and are so scriptural that they are made up almost entirely of scriptural language; references to which he has thrown into the margin. Few better liturgies probably exist."*

In transferring to our pages the Reformed Liturgy, we have reduced its somewhat unreasonable dimensions, by the preference of those shorter prayers which are furnished " where brevity is necessary," to the more expanded forms; and by some further abridgment where it has seemed needful.

* ORME'S *Life*, etc., p. 748.

THE ORDINARY PUBLIC WORSHIP ON THE LORD'S DAY.

The congregation being reverently composed, let the minister first crave God's assistance and acceptance of the Worship, to be performed in these or the like words :

O Eternal, Almighty, and most gracious GOD! heaven is thy throne, and earth is thy footstool; holy and reverend is thy name; thou art praised by the heavenly hosts, and in the congregation of thy saints on earth; and wilt be sanctified in all that come nigh unto thee. We are sinful and unworthy dust; but being invited by thee, are bold, through our blessed Mediator, to present ourselves and our supplications before thee. Receive us graciously, help us by thy Spirit; let thy fear be upon us; put thy laws into our hearts, and write them in our minds; let thy word come unto us in power, and be received in love, with attentive, reverent, and obedient minds. Make it to us the savour of life unto life. Cause us to be fervent in prayer, and joyful in thy praises, and to serve thee this day without distraction: that we may find that a day in thy courts is better than a thousand, and that it is good for us to draw near to GOD; through JESUS CHRIST our Lord and Saviour.   Amen.

Next, let one of the Creeds be read by the minister, saying :

In the profession of this Christian Faith we are here assembled.

I believe in God the Father, etc.

I believe in one God, etc.

And sometimes Athanasius' Creed.

THE TEN COMMANDMENTS.

GOD spake these words, and said, etc.

For the right informing and affecting the people, and moving them to a penitent believing Confession, some of these Sentences may be read.

By one man sin entered into the world, and death by sin, and so death passed upon all men, for that all have sinned.

For all have sinned, and come short of the glory of GOD.

GOD so loved the world, that he gave his only-begotten Son, that whosoever believeth in him, should not perish, but have everlasting life.

He that believeth on Him shall not be condemned, but he that believeth not is condemned already, because he hath not believed in the name of the only-begotten Son of GOD.

CHRIST hath redeemed us from the curse of the law, being made a curse for us.

Verily, I say unto you, Except ye be converted and become as little children, ye shall not enter into the kingdom of heaven.

Say unto them, As I live, saith the LORD GOD, I have no pleasure in the death of the wicked; but that the wicked turn from his way and live: Turn ye, turn ye from your evil ways; for why will ye die, O house of Israel?

I say unto you, there is joy in the presence of the angels of GOD, over a sinner that repenteth.

I will arise and go to my father, and say unto him, Father, I have sinned against heaven, and before thee, and am no more worthy to be called thy son.

THE CONFESSION OF SIN, AND PRAYER FOR PARDON AND SANCTIFICATION.

O most great, most just and gracious GOD: thou art of purer eyes than to behold iniquity, thou condemnest the ungodly, impenitent, and unbelievers; but hast promised mercy, through JESUS CHRIST, to all that repent and believe in him. We confess that we were conceived in sin, and are by nature children of wrath; and have all sinned and come short of the glory of GOD. We have neglected and abused thy holy worship, thy holy name, and thy holy day. We have dealt unjustly and uncharitably with our neighbours, not loving them as ourselves, nor doing to others as we would they should do to us. We have not sought first thy kingdom and righteousness, and been contented with our daily bread, but have been careful and troubled about many things, neglecting the one thing needful. Thou hast revealed thy wonderful love to us in CHRIST, and offered us pardon and salvation in him: but we have made light of it, and neglected so great salvation, and resisted thy Spirit, word, and ministers, and turned not at thy reproof: we have run into temptations; and the sin which we should have hated, we have committed in thy sight, both secretly and openly, ignorantly and carelessly, rashly and presumptuously, against thy precepts, thy promises and threats, thy mercies and thy judgments. Our transgressions are multiplied before thee, and our sins testify against

us ; if thou deal with us as we deserve, thou wilt
cast us away from thy presence into hell, where
the worm never dieth, and the fire is not quenched.
But in thy mercy, thy Son, and thy promises is
our hope. Have mercy upon us, most merciful
Father! Be reconciled to us, and let the blood
of JESUS CHRIST cleanse us from all our sins.
Take us for thy children, and give us the Spirit of
thy Son. Sanctify us wholly, shed abroad thy
love in our hearts, and cause us to love thee with
all our hearts. O make thy face to shine upon
thy servants ; save us from our sins, and from the
wrath to come ; make us a peculiar people to thee,
zealous of good works, that we may please thee,
and show forth thy praise. Help us to redeem
the time, and give all diligence to make our
calling and election sure. Give us things necessary
for thy service, and keep us from sinful discontent
and cares. And seeing all these things must be
dissolved, let us consider what manner of persons
we ought to be, in all holy conversation and
godliness. Help us to watch against temptations,
and resist and overcome the flesh, the devil, and
the world ; and being delivered out of the hand
of all our enemies, let us serve thee without fear, in
holiness and righteousness before thee all the days

of our life. Guide us by thy counsel, and after receive us into thy glory, through JESUS CHRIST our only Saviour. Amen.

Our Father which art in heaven, etc.

For the strengthening of faith, and raising the Penitent, some of these Sentences of the Gospel may be here read.

Hear what the Lord saith to the Absolution and Comfort of Penitent Believers.

The LORD your GOD is gracious and merciful, and will not turn away his face from you, if ye return unto him.

If any man sin, we have an advocate with the Father, JESUS CHRIST the righteous, and he is the propitiation for our sins, and not for ours only, but also for the sins of the whole world.

Be it known unto you, men and brethren, that through this man is preached to you the forgiveness of sins; and by him all that believe are justified from all things, from which they could not be justified by the law of Moses.

Come unto me, all ye that labour and are heavy laden, and I will give you rest. Take my yoke upon you, and learn of me, for I am meek and

N

lowly in heart, and ye shall find rest unto your souls. For my yoke is easy, and my burden is light.

Whosoever will, let him take of the water of life freely.

All that the Father hath given me, shall come to me; and him that cometh to me, I will in no wise cast out.

I will be merciful to their unrighteousness, and their sins and iniquities I will remember no more.

Hear also what you must be and do for the time to come, if you would be saved.

If any man be in Christ, he is a new creature; old things are passed away, behold all things are become new.

There is no condemnation to them that are in CHRIST JESUS, who walk not after the flesh, but after the Spirit. For they that are after the flesh, do mind the things of the flesh; but they that are after the Spirit, the things of the Spirit.

The fruit of the Spirit is love, joy, peace, long-suffering, gentleness, goodness, faith, meekness, temperance; against such there is no law. And they that are CHRIST'S, have crucified the flesh with the affections and lusts.

Love not the world, neither the things that are

in the world ; if any man love the world, the love
of the Father is not in him.   For all that is in
the world, the lust of the flesh, the lust of the eye,
and the pride of life, is not of the Father, but is
of the world.

For the grace of GOD that bringeth salvation,
hath appeared unto all men, teaching us that,
denying ungodliness and worldly lusts, we should
live soberly, and righteously, and godly, in this
present world ; looking for the blessed hope, and
the glorious appearing of the great GOD and our
Saviour JESUS CHRIST ; who gave himself for
us, that he might redeem us from all iniquity, and
purify to himself a peculiar people, zealous of
good works.

Therefore, my beloved brethren, be ye steadfast,
unmovable, always abounding in the work of the
LORD, forasmuch as ye know that your labour
is not in vain in the LORD.

*Then may be said the ninety-fifth or the hundredth
Psalm, or the eighty-fourth.*

*And next the Psalms in order for the day ; and
next shall be read a chapter of the Old Testament,
such as the minister findeth most seasonable ; or*

with the liberty expressed in the admonition before the second book of Homilies.

After which may be sung a Psalm, or the Te Deum said; then shall be read a chapter of the New Testament, and then the Prayer for the King and Magistrates. And after that, the sixty-seventh, or ninety-eighth, or some other Psalm, may be sung or said, or the Benedictus, or Magnificat. And the same order to be observed at the Evening Worship, if time allow it.

Next after the Psalm the Minister shall (in the pulpit) first reverently, prudently, and fervently pray, according to the state and necessities of the Church, and those especially that are present, and according to the subject that he is to preach on. And after Prayer, he shall preach upon some text of Holy Scripture, suiting his matter to the necessities of the hearers, and the manner of delivery to their quality and benefit.

After Sermon he shall pray for a blessing on the word of instruction and exhortation, which was delivered; and in his Prayers (before or after Sermon) ordinarily he shall pray for the conversion of Heathens, Jews, and other infidels; the subversion of idolatry, infidelity, Mahometanism, heresy, papal tyranny and superstition, schism and profaneness, and for the free progress of the Gospel, the increase of faith and godliness, the honouring of GOD's name, the enlargement of the kingdom of CHRIST, and the obedience of his saints through the nations of the earth. And in special for these nations; for the King's Majesty, and the rest of the Royal Family, for the Lords of his Majesty's Council, the Judges and other Magistrates of the land, for the Pastors of the Church, and all Congregations committed to their care and government. Always taking heed that no mixtures of imprudent, disorderly expressions, of private discontent and passion, of unreverent, disobedient, seditious, or factious intimations, tending to corrupt, and not to edify the people's minds, do turn either prayer or preaching into sin. And ordinarily in Church-communion, especially on the LORD's-day (which is purposely separated for the joyful commemoration of the blessed work of man's redemption), a considerable proportion of the public worship must consist of thanksgiving and praises to GOD, especially for JESUS CHRIST, and his benefits; still leaving it to the Minister's discretion to abbreviate some parts of worship, when he seeth it needful to be longer on some other.

THE GENERAL PRAYER.

O most holy, blessed, and glorious Trinity, Father, Son, and Holy Ghost, Three Persons and One GOD, our Creator, Redeemer, and Sanctifier, our LORD, our Governor and Father, hear us, and have mercy upon us, miserable sinners.

O LORD our Saviour, GOD and man! who, having assumed our nature, by thy sufferings, and death, and burial, wast made a ransom to take away the sins of the world; who being raised from the dead, ascended and glorified, art made Head over all things to the Church, which thou gatherest, justifiest, sanctifiest, rulest, and preservest, and which at thy coming thou wilt raise and judge to endless glory: We beseech thee to hear us, miserable sinners.

Make sure to us our calling and election, our unfeigned faith and repentance; that being justified, and made the sons of GOD, we may have peace with him, as our reconciled GOD and Father.

Let thy Holy Spirit sanctify us, and dwell in us, and cause us to deny ourselves, and to give up ourselves entirely to thee, as being not our own, but thine.

As the world was created for thy glory, let thy

name be glorified throughout the world; let self-love, and pride, and vain-glory be destroyed; cause us to love thee, fear thee, and trust in thee with all our hearts, and to live to thee.

Let all the earth subject themselves to thee, their King. Let the kingdoms of the world become the kingdoms of the LORD, and of his CHRIST. Let the atheists, idolaters, Mahometans, Jews, and other infidels, and ungodly people, be converted. Send forth meet labourers into the harvest, and let the Gospel be preached throughout all the world. Preserve and bless them in thy work. Sustain in patience, and seasonably deliver the churches that are oppressed by idolaters, infidels, Mahometans, or other enemies, or by the Roman Papal usurpations.

Unite all Christians in JESUS CHRIST, the true and only universal Head, in the true Christian and Catholic Faith and Love; cast out heresies and corruptions, heal divisions, let the strong receive the weak, and bear their infirmities; restrain the spirit of pride and cruelty, and let nothing be done in strife, or vain-glory.

Keep us from atheism, idolatry, and rebellion against thee; from infidelity, ungodliness, and sensuality; from security, presumption, and despair. Let us delight to please thee, and let thy word be the rule of our faith and lives; let us love it, and understand it, and meditate in it day and night.

Let us not corrupt or neglect thy worship; nor take thy holy Name in vain. Keep us from blasphemy, perjury, profane swearing, lying, contempt of thy ordinances, and from false, unworthy, and unreverent thoughts and speeches of GOD, or holy things; and from the neglect and profanation of thy holy day.

Put it into the hearts of the Kings and Rulers of the world to submit to CHRIST, and rule for him as nursing fathers to his Church; and save them from the temptations that would drown them in sensuality; or would break them upon CHRIST as a rock of offence, by engaging them against his holy doctrine, ways, and servants.

Have mercy on thy servant CHARLES, our king, protect his person, illuminate and sanctify him by thy Spirit, that above all things he may seek thine honour, the increase of faith, and holy obedience to thy laws; and may govern us as thy minister, appointed by thee for the terror of evildoers, and the praise of them that do well; that under him we may live a quiet and peaceable life, in all godliness and honesty.

Have mercy upon all the Royal Family, upon the Lords of the Council, and all the Nobility, the Judges, and other Magistrates of these lands. Let them fear thee, and be ensamples of piety and temperance, haters of injustice, covetousness, and pride, and defenders of the innocent: in their eyes let a vile person be contemned, but let them honour them that fear the LORD.

Let every soul be subject to the higher powers, and not resist; let them obey the king, and all in authority, not only for wrath, but for conscience' sake.

Give all the Churches able, holy, faithful pastors, that may soundly and diligently preach thy word, and guide the flocks in ways of holiness and peace, overseeing and ruling them not by constraint, but willingly, not for filthy lucre, but of a ready mind; not as being lords over thy heritage, but the servants of all, and ensamples to the flock; that when the chief Pastor shall appear, they may receive the crown of glory.

Let the people know those that are over them in the LORD, and labour among them preaching to them the word of GOD; let them highly esteem them in love for their works' sake, account them worthy of double honour, and obey them in the LORD.

Let parents bring up their children in holy nurture, that they may remember their Creator in the days of their youth; and let children love, honour, and obey them.   Let husbands love their wives, and guide them in knowledge and holiness; and let wives love and obey their husbands.   Let masters rule their servants in thy fear, and servants obey their masters in the LORD.

Keep us from murders, and violence, and injurious passionate words and actions.

Keep us from fornication and all uncleanness, from chambering and wantonness, from lustful thoughts and filthy communications, and all unchaste behaviour.

Keep us from stealing, or wronging our neighbour in his property, from perverting justice, from false witnessing and deceit, from slandering, backbiting, uncharitable censuring, or other wrong to the reputation of our neighbours.

Keep us from coveting anything that is our neighbours'.   Let us love our neighbours as ourselves, and do to others as we would they should do to us.

Cause us to love CHRIST in his members with a pure and fervent love, and to love our enemies, and do good to all, as we are able; but especially to the household of faith.

Give us our necessary sustentation and provision for thy service, and contentedness therewith; bless our labours, and the fruits of the earth in their season, and give us such temperate weather as tendeth hereunto. Deliver us and all thy servants from such sickness, wants, and other distresses, as may unseasonably take us off thy service. Keep us from gluttony and drunkenness, slothfulness, unlawful gain, and from making provision for the flesh to satisfy its lusts.

When we sin, restore us by true repentance and faith in CHRIST; let us loathe ourselves for our transgressions; forgive them all and accept us in thy well-beloved Son; save us from the curse and punishment which they deserve, and teach us heartily to forgive others; convert our enemies, persecutors and slanderers, and forgive them.

Cause us to watch against temptations, to resist and overcome the flesh, the devil, and the world; and by no allurements of pleasure, profit, or honour, to be drawn from thee to sin; let us patiently suffer with CHRIST, that we may reign with him.

Deliver us and all thy people from the enmity and rage of Satan and all his wicked instruments; and preserve us to thy heavenly kingdom.

For thou only art the universal King; all power is thine in heaven and earth; of thee, and through thee, and to thee are all things, and the glory shall be thine for ever. Amen.

The Sermon and Prayer being ended, let the minister dismiss the congregation with a Benediction, in these or the like words :—

Blessed are they that hear the word of GOD, and keep it.

The LORD bless you, and keep you; the LORD make his face to shine upon you, and be gracious unto you; the LORD lift up his countenance upon you, and give you peace.

The grace of our Lord JESUS CHRIST, and the love of GOD the Father, and the communion of the HOLY GHOST, be with you all. Amen.

A THANKSGIVING FOR CHRIST AND HIS GRACIOUS BENEFITS.

Most glorious GOD, accept, through thy beloved Son, though from the hands of sinners, the

thanksgiving which thy unspeakable love and
mercies, as well as thy command, do bind us to
offer up unto thee. Thou art the Father of
mercies, and the GOD of all consolation, full of
compassion, gracious, long-suffering, plenteous in
goodness and truth, keeping mercy for thousands,
forgiving iniquity, transgression, and sin. For
thy glory thou didst create us after thine image;
thou madest us a little lower than the angels, and
crownedst us with glory and honour, giving us
dominion over the works of thy hands, and put-
ting all these things under our feet. And when
we forsook thee, and broke thy covenant, and
rebelled against thee, and corrupted ourselves,
and turned our glory into shame; thou didst not
leave us in the hands of death, nor cast us out
into utter desperation: but thou didst so love the
sinful world, as to give thy Son to be our Saviour.
He took not upon him the nature of angels, but
of man: the Word was made flesh, and dwelt
among us. This is the unsearchable mystery of
love which the angels desire to pry into: he was
tempted, that he might succour them that are
tempted, and conquered the tempter, that had
conquered us; he became poor that was LORD of
all, to make us rich. He did no sin, but fulfilled

all righteousness, to save us from our unrighteousness. He made himself of no reputation, but was reviled, scorned, and spit upon, enduring the cross, and despising the shame, to cover our shame, and to bring us unto glory: thou laidst upon Him the iniquity of us all. He was bruised and wounded for our transgressions, that we might be healed by His stripes. He gave himself a ransom for us, and died for our sins, and rose again for our justification. We thank thee for His death that saveth us from death, and that He bore the curse to redeem us from the curse; and for His life which opened to us the way to life. Thou hast given Him to be Head over all things to the Church, and hast given the heathen to be His inheritance, and given Him a name above every name, and given all power and judgment unto Him. We thank thee for the new and better covenant, for thy great and precious promises: That thou hast given us eternal life in CHRIST. That we have the clear and sure revelation of thy will in the Holy Scriptures. That thou foundest thy Church upon apostles and prophets, JESUS CHRIST himself being the head corner-stone. And hast committed to thy ministers the word of reconciliation, that as ambassadors speaking in the stead of CHRIST, they might beseech us to be reconciled unto thee. We thank thee that by them thou hast opened our eyes, and turned us from darkness unto light, and from the power of Satan unto GOD. All thy paths, O LORD, are mercy and truth to such as keep thy covenant. We come into thy house in the multitude of thy mercies: O give thanks unto the LORD, for he is good, for His mercy endureth for ever. Glory ye in His holy name, let the hearts of them rejoice that seek Him. Blessed are the people that know the joyful sound; they shall walk, O LORD, in the light of thy countenance. In thy name they shall rejoice all the day, and in thy righteousness and favour shall they be exalted; blessed are they that dwell in thy house, they will be still praising thee. O satisfy us early with thy mercy, that we may rejoice and be glad in thee all our days. Guide us by thy counsel, and afterwards receive us unto thy glory; where, with all the blessed host of heaven, we may behold, admire, and perfectly and joyfully praise thee, our most glorious Creator, Redeemer, and Sanctifier, for ever and for ever. Amen.

X.

The Calvinistic Forms in the Book of Common Prayer.

"Though thousands were debtors to him [Calvin], as touching Divine knowledge, yet he to none, only to God."—HOOKER.

OF the many weighty treatises which have been written on the Book of Common Prayer, there are but few that do justice to the part taken by the Protestant divines of the Continent in its compilation. Admirers of the breviary and missal, delighting to trace the correspondence of their Liturgy with mediæval forms, are apt to omit all reference to these more modern sources. Even where their ingenuity is puzzled to find analogy for its offices in Romish or Eastern sacramentaries, they will laboriously avoid recognition of the true but despised origin. Yet the fact is established beyond question, that several of the Foreign Reformers shared in the authorship or revision of the English Prayer Book. Calvin, Knox, Luther, Melancthon, Bucer, Martyr, were engaged in the work; and to their aid must be traced some of its finest passages.

Melancthon and Bucer were indeed the authors of no inconsiderable portion of the Anglican forms. In 1543, those Reformers drew up a system of doctrine and worship for the Protestant Archbishopric of Cologne. This they did at the solicitation of Hermann, "that pious Confessor, late Elector and Archbishop of Colen, who, for adhering to the Protestant religion, and setting on foot the Reformation of his country, was deprived by the Pope and Emperor."* The work which they thus prepared, was published in Latin at Bonn, in 1545, under the title, "*Nostra Hermanni Archepisc. Coloniensis Simplex et Pia Deliberatio et Christiana in Verbo Dei fundata Reformatio.*" A translation was published at London, 1547, entitled "Reformation of Doctrine," etc.

The Liturgy of Cologne was in the hands of the English Reformers when they were engaged upon the Book of Common Prayer; and "from this Liturgy," says Archbishop Laurence, "our offices bear evident marks of having been freely borrowed—liberally imitating, but not servilely copying it."†

* STRYPE, *Eccl. Mem. Edw. VI.*
† LAURENCE *on the Thirty-nine Articles*, etc., pp. 377, 378.

o

From Bucer and Melancthon's Liturgy, the Baptismal offices of the Prayer Book are substantially taken. In the Communion service, the Confession of Sins, the Absolution and succeeding sentences, and the Thanksgiving in the Post-Communion service, are of similar origin.* Nearly the whole of the form of Solemnization of Matrimony will be found in the Cologne Ritual; and a large portion of the Order for the Burial of the Dead. The anthem, "O LORD GOD, most holy," etc., is from Luther.†

These are not the only traces of the Cologne Liturgy to be met with in the Anglican Prayer-Book: plainly showing in what estimation that formulary was held by the compilers, and what frequent reference they had to its excellent services. But although we may fairly claim the Liturgy of Cologne as a fruit of the Calvinistic Reformation,—for Bucer, who had the chief hand in it, was a disciple of Calvin,—our business for the present is more strictly with the Genevan divines; and we proceed to inquire what Calvin

---

* WARTER, *Teaching of the Prayer Book*, 104. The second of the Exhortations is extracted from a work of the Reformer PETER MARTYR. See *Liturgical Services*, etc., Parker Society, p. 186, *note*.
    † LAURENCE, 381.

and Knox contributed to the preparation of the Book of Common Prayer.

The Fathers of the English Reformation were far from entertaining those unfraternal sentiments towards the ministry and churches of Scotland and the Continent, which in our day disgrace the cause of Protestantism.   They acknowledged the claims of their Presbyterian brethren to respect and fellowship; and by advancing to office persons who had obtained Presbyterian orders, they gave practical evidence of this recognition. So Cranmer for many years reserved a chair in the university of Cambridge for the illustrious Melancthon, hoping that he might be attracted to England.* So Martyr and Bucer were called to professorships at Oxford and Cambridge, and were consulted and appealed to on every important topic of ecclesiastical doctrine and discipline that arose during their residence.

When, in the year 1551, John Knox visited England, he was invited to assist in the revision of the Prayer Book, then in progress.†   There were, doubtless, many parts of that formulary which

* Rev. Dr. BUTLER, *The Common Prayer Book Interpreted*, p. 56.
† KNOX had already been appointed one of the chaplains of EDWARD VI.—STRYPE's *Cranmer*, 299.

must have been repugnant to the severe judgment of the Scotch Reformer: but it was not to be expected that all his suggestions would be followed out. So much influence, however, had he among the revisors, that he procured an important change in the Communion Service: completely excluding the notion of the real presence in the sacrament.* The following year, he was employed on a revision of the Articles of Religion, previous to their ratification by act of Parliament. †

Calvin, too, was consulted in the compilation of the Prayer Book; and, though not so directly engaged upon it, was the author of several of its forms. The introductory portion of the daily service is due to him. According to the first Book of Edward VI., that service began with the Lord's Prayer. ‡　The foreign Reformers consulted, § recommended the insertion of some preliminary forms; and hence the origin of the Sentences, the Exhortation, the Confession, and the Absolu-

---

　* M'CRIE's *Life of Knox*, pp. 67, 68.

　† STRYPE's *Cranmer*, p. 273.

　‡ *Liturgies of King Edward VI.*, Parker Society, 1844.— CARDWELL's *Two Liturgies of Edward VI.*

　§ BISHOP BROWNELL's *Comm. on the Prayer Book*, p. 73. These Reformers were Peter Martyr and Martin Bucer, who were then in England. SHORT's *Hist. of the Church of England*, p. 281.

tion.   These elements were borrowed, not from
any ancient formulary, but from a ritual drawn up
by Calvin for the Church at Strasburg.*   They
" were taken in great part," says an Episcopalian
writer, "from a Liturgy composed by Calvin.
The Ten Commandments were also introduced
into the Communion Service, probably from the
same source."†   We may add that the Responses
which follow the rehearsal of the Commandments
in that service, are taken from Pollanus, who
translated the Strasburg Liturgy, and published
it at London in 1556.‡

To diminish the credit due to the compilers of
the Prayer Book for this judicious and liberal use
of Calvin's Liturgy, it has been urged that their
selection was confined to the introductory and
subsidiary parts of Divine worship.   We shall
only specify, in answer, a *seventh* instance of their
indebtedness to the Calvinistic Forms.   The very
words of the distribution of the sacred elements,
in the celebration of the LORD's Supper, are taken

---

* *La Forme des Prières et Chants Ecclésiastiques.* Strasbourg,
1545, 8vo.   See a *Notice sur la Vie et les Ouvrages de Calvin*, in the
third volume of LA FRANCE PROTESTANTE : Paris, 1853.

† *The Common Prayer Book Interpreted*, p. 55.

‡ See Archbishop LAURENCE's *Sermons on the Thirty-nine Articles*,
p. 209 ; and STRYPE's *Eccl. Mem. Edw. VI.*, b. i. c. 29.

from a Calvinistic Liturgy: that of the distinguished A'Lasco, who derived it chiefly from the Liturgy of Strasburg. The sentences, "Take and eat this," etc., "Drink this," etc., were "suggested," says an Episcopalian writer, " from the ritual of a church of foreigners then resident in England, who were most remarkable for their rejection of ancient practices."*

" The truth is," observes Jeremy Taylor, " that although they framed the Liturgy with the greatest consideration that could be, by all the united wisdom of Church and State, yet, as if prophetically to avoid their being charged by after ages with a *crepusculum* of religion—a dark, twilight, imperfect Reformation—they joined to their own star all the shining tapers of the other reformed churches, calling for the advice of the eminently learned and zealous Reformers in other kingdoms, that the light of all together might show them a clear path to walk in."†

It is curious, and not a little amusing, to observe the treatment which these Calvinistic portions of the Prayer Book receive at the hands of High

* Rev. Dr. BUTLER, *The Common Prayer Book Interpreted*, p. 128. See also CARDWELL's *Hist. of Conferences*, p. 6.

† Bishop TAYLOR's *Works*, vii. 288. Butler.

Church ritualists. Their object being to make out, as far as possible, the remote antiquity of its forms, they seek for each of them some parallel in Roman or Eastern liturgies. Wherever they can trace similarity of use and resemblance of form, they infer, not unreasonably, a designed imitation. Only when successful in tracing back a form to " Catholic usage," is their critical search satisfied. But in approaching these Calvinistic innovations, our ritualist is sadly at fault. Loath to refer them to their unmistakeable sources, he takes a new journey into the past, and overhauls his accumulated stores of missals, pontificats, and sacramentaries, but comes back with nothing that ingenuity can twist into a resemblance of paternity. We shrink from the cruelty of informing him at last, that these forms are the offspring of a system which, however venerated by his fathers,* is identified to his mind with heresy, false doctrine, and schism, from which he piously prays, " Deliver us."

We have said that no ancient Liturgy opens with a general confession of sins and supplication of

---

* " A Nursery unto GOD," is the title given by Archbishop Grindal to the city of Geneva.

forgiveness.* The Anglican ritual, at the beginning of each of its chief services, the Common Prayer and the Communion, presents this feature. Without analogy elsewhere, it finds a parallel in the Liturgies of the Reformed Churches. Tractarian authors, warned perhaps by intuitive suspicion of its origin, deplore the insertion. Not less do they lament the introduction of the Decalogue in the Communion Office. But though these elements of the Protestant Episcopal worship may have no warrant in "Catholic usage," they are to us significant memorials of a state of amity once existing between the Church of England and the Protestant communions on the Continent.

There was certainly on the part of the English Reformers, no lack of willingness to transcribe those customs which were commendable in other Protestant Churches. We have seen how, in 1563, Archbishop Grindal translated from Calvin's Liturgy the form of prayer used during a visitation

* Consult PALMER'S *Origines Liturgicæ :* BRETT.

"Great interest attaches to that [Calvin's] Confession, since from its position, as well as its wording, it manifestly gave occasion to the General Confession of our own Prayer Book."—*Private Prayers in the reign of Queen Elizabeth,* Parker Society, p. 488, *note.* See LAURENCE'S *Bampton Lectures,* pp. 207, 208.

of the Plague ; a form which became the model of other similar services in after years.* Near the same period we find Bishop Pilkington enjoining the use of Calvin's Daily Prayers at Rivington School, instituted and founded by him.† The Liturgy of John Knox was then, and continued long after, in common use, as a manual of private devotion. Under the form of a collection of " Christian Prayers and Godly Meditations," it had been published in 1569, by royal authority.‡ Only a few years later, it became customary to print, by authority, the Calvinistic Prayers, together with the Psalms in metre, as an appendix to the Bible ; in some editions of which we find the Common Prayer prefixed to the Sacred Books, while Knox's Liturgy is appended. This re-markable feature may be observed in Bibles

* Vide p. 155.

† BISHOP PILKINGTON, *Works*, p. 671.

‡ " *Christian Prayers and Meditations*," London, 1569. A copy of this very rare book is in the possession of the Rev. Dr. Bethune, New York. It is republished in the Parker Society's volume of " Private Prayers," pp. 429—561. These Prayers comprise almost the whole of Calvin and Knox's Liturgies, intermingled with the Litany and various collects. A special edition of them, most skilfully ornamented in the style of the ancient books of devotion, was printed in 1578, for the private use of Queen Elizabeth ; hence it was designated " The Queen's Prayer Book."

printed as early as the year 1596, and as late as 1640.*

The practice of singing metrical psalms, introduced about this time, was also borrowed from the Calvinistic worship; it became popular at once. and has continued to form an important part of religious observance.†

The Catechism for Children, now in use, was compiled by Cranmer in 1548, and taken chiefly from a Lutheran formulary.‡   Previous to this, the Catechism of Erasmus had been introduced, and in 1547 was ordered to be used at Winchester College and elsewhere.   Calvin's Catechism, however, soon came into general use, and in 1578 was

* BARKER's Bible of 1590, small quarto, black letter, with notes.   The same, of 1640, octavo, with references.—*Library of the American Bible Society*.

The following are the titles of the Calvinistic Prayers appended to these editions: "A Forme of Prayer to be used in private houses every morning and evening.   Morning Prayer.   Evening Prayer. A Godly Prayer to be said at all times.   A Confession for all estates and times.   (Conf. of Sins.)   A Prayer to be said before a man begins his work.   A Prayer for the whole estate of CHRIST's Church."

† "The —— day of September [1559] the new Morning Prayers began now first at St. Antholin's in Bridge-row, ringing at five in the morning; and then a Psalm was sung, as was used among the Protestants of Geneva, all men, women, and young folks singing together; which custom was about this time brought also into St. Paul's."—STRYPE's *Life of Archbishop Grindal*, b. i. c. 3.

‡ WARTER *on the Prayer Book*.

ordered by statute to be used at the University of Oxford.*

A custom which, at first glance, would appear almost incompatible with the Anglican system, was in the year 1572 adopted and established by ecclesiastical law. We refer to those meetings of the clergy for conference and religious improvement, which were termed Exercises or Prophesyings. This feature of Calvinism had been borrowed by the Church of Scotland as early as 1560.† It was established and regulated by the First Book of Discipline; whence the "directions" issued in various dioceses of the Church of England were evidently drawn.‡   These meetings received the countenance of Parker, Chaderton, Parkhurst, and in fact most of the English prelates, who found much good to arise from their prevalence.§ Some incidental abuses, however, having been

---

* CARDWELL'S *Doc. Annals of the Church of England*, vol. i. p. 300, *note*.

† *The First Book of Discipline*, ch. xii. DUNLOP'S *Confessions*, ii. 587.

‡ CARDWELL'S *Doc. Annals of the Church of England*, vol. i. p. 389. "The practice had been adopted in the first instance in Scotland, and rules had been provided for it by the Convention [Council] of 1560," p. 390, *note*.

§ "Exercises among the ministers and curates of churches, called Prophesyings, from the Apostle's word, 1 Cor. xiv., were now used in most dioceses."—STRYPE'S *Annals*, vol. ii. p. 472.

alleged against the practice, as that " laymen and Nonconforming ministers were allowed to take part in the debates; that speeches had been made against the government and the services of the Church;"* the Queen was led, in 1577, to issue an order for the complete suppression of the "exercise called ' Prophesying.' "† Great grief was felt, upon this arbitrary proceeding, by the most pious and eminent ministers of England; and his refusal to concur in it was the occasion upon which the excellent Grindal, then Archbishop of Canterbury, lost the favour of his royal mistress.‡ At a later period, Lord Bacon, in a letter to King James, questioned whether it were not advisable to renew an exercise which had been practised in the Church for some years, and had been suppressed in opposition to the opinion of "the greatest and gravest prelate of the land."§

Thus did the Reformers of England, anxious not only to embellish their own purified system of religion, but also to establish its harmony with

* STRYPE'S *Grindal*, p. 326. NEAL'S *Puritans*, vol. i. p. 231.

† *Queen Elizabeth's Letter to the Bishops*, etc. CARDWELL, i. 428.

‡ *Life and Remains of Grindal.*

§ *Works*, vol. i. p. 357.—*Considerations touching the pacification of the Church of England.*

others, adopt many of the prominent excellencies of our own Calvinistic worship. Some of those features have been removed, but others remain. The opening services of the Common Prayer and the Communion are still retained, with the full stamp of their Presbyterian origin upon them. Those kindly sympathies which they commemorate have long since ceased to flow; and a brazen wall of separation has been erected by the bigotry of ages to shut out from the tender mercies of Episcopacy all Protestant Communions. The Churches of the Reformation, so frequently and so affectionately named in the times of Cranmer, and Grindal, and Hooker, are now seldom spoken of but with opprobrium. The advances of their sisterly affection are generally repulsed with over-bearing arrogance. Their worship is despised, their orders are a theme of jest, their struggles and sufferings* viewed with indifference or contempt. Yet, whenever as strangers we kneel at the altars

* When intelligence of the Massacre of St. Bartholomew's Eve (August 24th, 1572) reached England, a form of penitential and intercessory prayer was appointed to be observed in all the Churches, on account of the afflictions undergone by the Protestant brethren in France. See STRYPE's *Parker*, ii. 131; CARDWELL, i. 374, *note*. Would any such disaster to the Churches of Protestantism in our day elicit from the same source a token of sympathy, or a word of regret? [In reference to this note and the text, see Editor's Preface.]

of this unfriendly Church, and listen to these forms of Scripture sentence and commandment, of confession and absolution, we seem to hear again the welcome of Christian recognition, which the Fathers of our system received, when they joined the Reformers of England in works of faith and labours of love.

XI.

Liturgy of the Reformed Dutch Church.

"Antiquity, while it adds weight to a ritual composed even of sacred elements, adds yet more to one whose composition is essentially human. Such a Liturgy should be re-touched only at long intervals, and with great circumspection by the Church."

VINET. *Past. Theology.*

WE approach this branch of our subject with the more interest and satisfaction, because of all the Calvinistic Churches represented in these United States, the Reformed Dutch denomination alone has faithfully retained her ancient forms of worship. The earliest member of the Presbyterian family transplanted to these Western shores, she exhibits to us in this respect more perfectly than any other the natural outgrowth of the system from which she sprung. But besides preserving thus far inviolate a formulary handed down from the first days of the Reformation, the Reformed Dutch Church bears also, at the present moment, an aspect of peculiar hopefulness and promise for the future. The subject of a re-arrangement of that ritual, which in some of its offices has become virtually obsolete, because unsuited to the requirements of the times, is now receiving serious consideration from a committee under appointment of the General Synod; and will probably be acted upon in the course of a very few months. To this quarter, then, the advocates of improvement in the worship of our churches may look, with some definite expectation, for a fulfilment of the great desideratum of a Presbyterian Liturgy.

The Liturgy of the Church of Holland is, with a few trifling exceptions, completely and accurately rendered in our American translation.* It may be divided into two parts: of which the one is a collection of prayers for the ordinary services of worship; and the other, of Forms in the administration of the Sacraments and Ordinances of religion.† The former of these divisions, or that which relates to the ordinary services of the Sabbath and week-day assemblies, has fallen into desuetude among the churches of this country; as

---

* We have noticed but two omissions; the one being a prayer in the marriage service, and the other an article on "The Consolation of the Sick."

† THE LITURGY OF THE REFORMED DUTCH CHURCH; or, the Forms used therein.—I. Christian Prayers to be used in the Assembly of the Faithful, and on other occasions. II. Administration of the Holy Sacraments. III. Church Discipline. IV. Ordination of Church officers. V. Celebration of Marriage. VI. Of Comforting the Sick.

indeed in Holland, where these forms went out of use toward the close of the seventeenth century, or contemporaneously with our own Scottish forms.* In fact, it may be doubted whether in this country they have ever been used at all. The deficiency has been supplied in part by a species of brief directory embodied in the Constitution of the American Church, under the head of "Customs and Usages." An examination of that directory will show, that notwithstanding the abandonment of the use of written prayers in the Sabbath services, there has not been a total relinquishment of the liturgical character of worship.† The main elements of the Calvinistic service are there

* T. D. W., in the *Chr. Intelligencer*, Nov. 5th, 1852.

† CONSTITUTION OF THE REFORMED DUTCH CHURCH OF NORTH AMERICA; Chapter III. "*Of Customs and Usages;*" Article I. Section 4th.

"For the purpose of uniformity in the order of worship, the following is to be observed by all the churches :—

"1st. After a space for private devotion, the minister shall introduce the public worship in the morning by invoking the Divine presence and blessing. 2nd. Salutation. 3rd. Reading the Ten Commandments, or some other portion of Scripture, or both. 4th. Singing. 5th. Prayer. 6th. Singing. 7th. Sermon. 8th. Prayer. 9th. Collection of Alms. 10th. Singing. 11th. Pronouncing the Apostolic Benediction.

"The order of the afternoon and evening services shall be the same as in the morning, excepting the reading of the Ten Commandments. The last service on the Lord's day shall conclude with the Christian Doxology."

P

retained, viz.: the Lord's Prayer, Ten Commandments, and Creed,* besides the features of a "Salutation" at the commencement of the service, and a Doxology at the close. In Holland universally, and in America to some extent, the clergy wear an official dress during the performance of their public functions.†

But while it is true that the forms of common prayer have thus fallen into disuse, what is perhaps more important, the administration of the sacraments and ordinances remains unimpaired, according to the original model of the Reformation. The Constitution of the Dutch Church enjoins upon ministers the use of the forms of Baptism, Communion, and Ordination ; which, accordingly, are celebrated to this day in the order and manner of their liturgical prescription.

It is contemplated in the revision now in process, to supply those deficiencies which render a portion

---

* We are not aware that the Creed is at present used in any of the Dutch Reformed Churches at the ordinary services of worship ; as it certainly was used until of late years. But it still occupies a conspicuous place in the Communion Office.

† We do not know whether it be the old *Geneva* gown that is worn at present in Holland, as it was until within a century past. The academic gown is used in this country. A writer in the *New Brunswick Review* for February, 1855, mentions the fact that during the celebration of the Communion, elders in the Churches of Holland wear a distinctive dress.

of this formulary unfit for present use, without material alteration of those parts which are still used. As it now stands, the Reformed Dutch Liturgy is, we believe, precisely what it was in the year 1619, and substantially as when first adopted in 1568. The greater part of its forms indeed date back to the year 1541, and like almost everything else in the ritual of the Reformed Churches, must be ascribed to the great Reformer Calvin.

A brief history of the compilation of this Liturgy may not be without interest to the reader. For the leading facts here given, we are indebted to the systematic and reliable work of the German ritualist Ebrard.*

In 1541, if not earlier, Calvin composed for the congregation to which he had ministered

---

* REFORMIRTES KIRCHENBUCH ; *Vollständige Sammlung der in der Reformirten Kirche eingeführten Kirchengebete und Formulare.* Von AUG. EBRARD, *Prof. der Theologie zu Zürich :* Zurich, 1847, 1 vol. small quarto, pp. 323. We are indebted, also, for some of the statements here given, to the author of two very valuable articles published in the *Christian Intelligencer* newspaper, New York, October 28th and November 4th, 1852, under the head of "The Liturgy and Forms of Worship." These articles, bearing the initials T. D. W., are attributed to the pen of the learned and excellent senior pastor of the Collegiate Reformed Dutch Church in the city of New York; than whom no better authority on the subject could be desired.

awhile at Strasburg, a form of worship, which was printed in 1545 at that city.* This formulary resembled closely his Liturgy of Geneva, but seems to have contained some features not to be found in that latter.† It lies at the foundation of the Dutch and German Reformed rituals ; and, as we have had occasion to notice elsewhere,‡ was the source of several portions of the English Book of Common Prayer.

In 1546, Valerandus Pollanus, successor of Calvin as minister of the congregation at Strasburg, published a liturgy for his people, which appears to have been identical with Calvin's. For, in 1551, having passed over with his flock to England, where they established themselves at Glastonbury, in Somersetshire, Pollanus published " a translation of Calvin's Liturgy of Strasburg," as it was used by his congregation. § It is this version that was used by Cranmer and

* In a preceding chapter we have referred to this document, which, however, it has not been our good fortune to possess. We find it described in the very thorough bibliographical notice of the works of Calvin, in volume third of the FRANCE PROTESTANTE, Paris, 1853.

† As, for instance, a form of Absolution after the Confession of Sins, in the service for the Lord's day.

‡ Vide p. 197.

§ *Private Prayers in the Reign of Queen Elizabeth:* Parker Society, 1851; p. 458, *note.* See STRYPE, *Mem.* II., i. 378, etc.

his colleagues in drawing up the Common Prayer Book.

Shortly after this publication, A'Lasco, the distinguished superintendent of the German and Walloon congregation, which had been formed at London,* prepared in Latin a Liturgy on the basis of that which Pollanus had translated from Calvin; and this composes the substance of the Holland Liturgy, as well as that of the Palatinate.†

A'Lasco's liturgy, thus founded on Pollanus's translation, was rendered into the Dutch language in 1556 by John Utenhoven, an eminent Christian layman of the period.‡ The Latin edition meanwhile was published at Frankfort in 1555, entitled,

* JOHN A'LASCO, a Roman Catholic Bishop, uncle to the king of Poland, converted to the Reformed faith, came to England in 1548, upon the invitation of Cranmer. He returned to Embden in Friesland, in 1549; but circumstances soon compelled his return to England, where he was appointed in July, 1556, superintendent of the foreign Protestant congregation, established at London. See Burnet and Strype.

† EBRARD'S *Ref. Kirchenbuch*, Preface, p. xxix.

‡ JOHN UTENHOVEN, a native of Ghent and a man of rank, was an elder and assistant to John A'Lasco, in the Walloon Church at London. See Strype, *Eccl. Mem. Edw. VI.*, b. i. c. 20. In 1549 he visited Zurich, when Bishop Hooper gave him letters to the celebrated Bullinger, introducing him as "a man illustrious both by his birth and virtues, most sincere in the true religion, and entirely opposed to all the mischiefs of sectarianism; he is, moreover, exceedingly intimate with Master John A'Lasco."—*Original Letters relative to the English Reformation :* Parker Society, Letter XXIX.

"The Form of Ecclesiastical Service in the German Church of foreigners, established at London in England."*

But before this, in 1554, an abridgment of A' Lasco's yet unpublished Liturgy had been made by Martin Micronius; and this was printed in the Dutch language at Embden, in Hanover, under the title, "Christian Ordinances of the Netherlands Congregations of CHRIST; with the approbation of the Ministers and Elders of the Church of CHRIST of the Low Dutch at London; diligently collected and arranged by Martin Micronius."†

A few farther modifications brought this formulary into its present shape. Composed originally by Calvin in French, translated by Pollanus into the English, re-arranged by A'Lasco in Latin, then translated by Utenhoven into the Dutch, and abridged by Micronius, it was finally reviewed by Dathenus, and adopted in 1566 as the standard of worship in the Reformed Church of Holland.

It was not, however, until the year 1574, that, by a decree of the Synod of Holland and Zealand,

* Forma ac tota ecclesiastici ministerii in peregrinorum, potissimum vero Germanorum Ecclesia, instituta Londini in Anglia."

† "*Christelicke Ordinantien der Nederlandschen Ghemeijnten Christi,*" etc. EBRARD.

this Liturgy was imposed as a prescribed service upon the churches. Having been already approved by the Synod of Wesel, it was in that year confirmed, and order was given that it be used by all the ministers. Some of the offices are of more modern date. The "Consolation of the Sick" was introduced in 1587; and the form of baptizing adults in 1604.

The numerous congregations of refugees from Holland which were formed in England during the Spanish persecution in that country,* used this order of worship. At one period of the reign of Queen Elizabeth, there were no fewer than eight congregations of Dutch Protestants in the city of London alone. The number diminished, however, before many years, and for more than a century there existed but one such congregation; now, we believe, entirely extinct.

The forms of worship peculiar to the Holland churches, which were observed at London, as well

---

* Great numbers of pious foreigners, Dutch and of other nations, were now in and about London; many whereof were driven out of their own countries by the Popish persecution. These had a place assigned them for their safe assembling themselves together for the public worship of GOD, being a large and fair part of the church of the Augustin friary dissolved."—STRYPE, *Eccl. Mem.*, *Edw.* VI., b. i. c. 29.

as in other towns of England, with the full approbation and sanction of the Anglican Reformers,
commended themselves, by their scriptural purity
and beauty, to the respect of all Protestant communions; and it is a curious fact, recorded in the
history of the Huguenots, that when, about the
middle of the eighteenth century, all assemblies
for worship, according to the rites of the French
Reformed Church, were forbidden, the Protestants
of Paris were accustomed to meet and celebrate
Divine service after the forms of the Church of
Holland; by which course they evaded the letter
of the law, and at the same time beautifully exemplified the harmony of these sister Churches in
their doctrines and ordinances.*

The Liturgy of the Reformed Dutch Church
was first translated into English for the use of
several English and Scottish congregations formed
in Holland.†   The translation now in use was
effected toward the latter part of the past century,
by the Rev. Dr. Livingston, and is remarkably
faithful and correct.

* De Felice, *History of the Protestants of France*, p. 523.
  † An edition published at Amsterdam, 1772, for the use of the
English Established Church in that city, is before us. It is bound
up with the metrical Psalms of David, by Tate and Brady.

As the larger portion of the Reformed Dutch Liturgy is derived from sources which have already been adduced, we content ourselves with two brief selections from it.* The following prayers from the Baptismal Service are the more interesting to us, because it is to be feared that in the present revision they will undergo modification, to suit the low conceptions of the value of this rite and the efficacy of the grace accompanying it, that prevail in the churches :†

INVOCATION.

O ALMIGHTY and Eternal GOD : We beseech thee that thou wilt be pleased, of thine infinite mercy, graciously to look upon these children; and incorporate them by thy HOLY SPIRIT into thy Son JESUS CHRIST : That they may be buried with him into his death, and be raised with him in newness of life : That they may daily follow

---

* The penitential tone pervades all the prayers of the Dutch Liturgy. Confession of sin and supplication for pardon occupy the chief place in every form. It is a singular fact, that the prayer which Calvin composed for a special fast (in 1541, "when Germany was infested both with war and pestilence," *Calv. Ep.*), took, in the Dutch Liturgy, the place of a regular Sunday morning supplication; thus giving a character of sorrow and dejection to the whole service throughout the year. We have quoted this prayer in full on p. 157.

† See **Editor's Preface.**

him, joyfully bearing their cross, and cleave unto him in true faith, firm hope, and ardent love: That they may, with a comfortable sense of thy favour, leave this life, which is nothing but a continual death; And that, at the last day, they may appear without terror before the judgment-seat of CHRIST thy Son: Through JESUS CHRIST our Lord, who with Thee and the HOLY GHOST, one only GOD, lives and reigns for ever. Amen.

THANKSGIVING.

ALMIGHTY GOD and merciful Father: We thank and praise thee, that thou hast forgiven us and our children all our sins, through the blood of thy beloved Son JESUS CHRIST; and received us through thy HOLY SPIRIT, as members of thy only begotten Son, and adopted us to be thy children, and sealed and confirmed the same unto us by holy baptism. We beseech thee, through the same Son of thy love, that thou wilt be pleased always to govern these baptized children by thy HOLY SPIRIT; that they may be piously and religiously educated, increase and grow up in the Lord JESUS CHRIST, that they then may acknowledge thy fatherly goodness and mercy, which thou hast shown to them and us; and live in all righteousness, under our only Teacher, King, and High Priest, JESUS CHRIST; and manfully fight against and overcome sin, the devil, and his whole dominion: To the end that they may eternally praise and magnify thee, and thy Son JESUS CHRIST, together with the HOLY GHOST, the one only true GOD. Amen.

On the whole, it will be readily acknowledged, that in her present Liturgy, the Reformed Dutch Church possesses an invaluable formulary of public devotion. Though defective as to the ordinary services of worship—which, however, are considerably in advance of the unmitigated baldness of our Scottish Presbyterian service—this ritual is sufficiently full in the more important offices of Baptism, Communion, and Ordination. And as these offices are not only furnished, but imposed, the Reformed Dutch Church can hardly be charged with neglecting to provide the food of devotion for those of her own household.

We confess to some apprehension in looking for the result of the present deliberations on the revision of the Reformed Dutch Liturgy. We are not without fear lest the desire of accommodating them to the low standard of the popular taste may lead to a sacrifice of the tone and spirit that pervade those ancient forms. We should infinitely prefer a simple return to the prayers of Calvin, Knox, and Baxter,* for the supply of what little is lacking; to an adjunction of purely modern and immature productions. We dread the incongruities of "new wine in old bottles," and "new cloth unto an old garment." But we shall hope for better things.

---

* Two suggestions may be pardoned in reference to the proposed amendment of the service for the morning of the LORD's Day. And, first, as to the use of the LORD's PRAYER: Its proper place, according to our modern arrangement, is at the close of the *first* prayer or Invocation. So long as the Calvinistic worship retained its *cumulative* order, the sermon occupying a central position, and the principal prayer occurring towards the close, it was proper that this Divine form should conclude the service. But this order has been practically broken by placing the "long prayer" before the sermon. Hence there is no longer a significance in locating the LORD's Prayer at the end.

The other suggestion relates to the APOSTLES' CREED. The ancient practice of the Dutch and Scottish Churches was (as it now is that of the Continental Churches), to rehearse the Creed not only on sacramental occasions, but in the principal service of the LORD's Day. Its place seems to be at the close of the *second* prayer; and, in fact, it was so used at first in the church of Geneva (see the *Notice sur la vie de Calvin*, already quoted), though afterwards transposed to the conclusion of the service. It has always been used as a *prayer* in the Calvinistic ritual, with a preface similar to that in the Dutch Reformed Communion Office.

XII.

Liturgy of the Palatinate.

"None, as I suppose, of sound judgment, will derogate from the Liturgy, if the form thereof be in all parts agreeable to the word of GOD, the example of the primitive Church, and that holy decency which St. Paul commendeth."—LORD BACON.

DISTINCT in some noteworthy particulars, though of kindred origin and general character, the Liturgy of the Palatinate deserves a brief notice separate from that of the Netherlands just considered. In the fertile and populous region of the Upper Rhine, whose plains and villages have so often suffered the devastations of war, Protestantism early gained a foothold, which for three centuries has been firmly maintained. It was in 1563 that the Elector Frederick III., " of blessed ancestral Christian memory,"* ordered the preparation and publication of a Liturgy, together with a summary of Christian doctrine," faithfully drawn from the pure word of GOD."†   The Re-

---

* Imprimatur of the Palatinate Liturgy published in 1684, by order of the Count Palatine Charles, quoted in an article of the *Mercersburg Review*, January, 1850, to which we are chiefly indebted for the translation of the prayers hereafter given.

† *Ibid.*

formers of Heidelberg, Ursinus, Olevianus, and
Tremellius,* were charged with the work of
drawing up this formulary of doctrine and devotion.† These theologians, being in close relations
of fraternity with the distinguished A'Lasco, who
had then recently published his Liturgy for the
Dutch congregation at London, took that work for
the basis of their compilation; which will be
found substantially to agree with the present
Dutch Reformed ritual, both having been drawn
from the same source. But while the Dutch
formulary has been subjected to three or four

* Two of these personages were eminent professors in the
University of Heidelberg, and each of them took a distinguished part
in the work of Reformation there. ZACHARY URSINUS was a native
of Silesia, a pupil of Melancthon, appointed in 1561 to the chair of
theology at Heidelberg; he died in 1583. GASPAR OLEVIANUS was
the son of a baker at Treves; he studied theology at Geneva, and
afterwards became minister at Heidelberg, where he died in 1583.
EMMANUEL TREMELLIUS, born at Ferrara, was of Jewish extraction;
he was converted by the instrumentality of Peter Martyr; and after
visiting Holland and England, where he was some time professor at
Cambridge, settled at Heidelberg, where he was appointed Hebrew
professor; he died in 1580.—ZURICH LETTERS, Parker Society, pp.
386, 450, note.

† EBRARD'S Reformirtes Kirchenbuch, pp. xxix., xxx. The doctrinal part of their work was the composition of the Palatine
Catechism, commonly called the Heidelberg Catechism; which was
adopted as the standard of the Church of Holland by the Synod of
Dort; early translated into English, and in 1591 published by
authority of the Church of Scotland for general use.—DUNLOP'S
Collection of Confessions, etc., of the Church of Scotland, Edinburgh,
1721; vol. ii. pp. 273–361.

processes of elimination, that of the Palatinate has probably preserved more of the original matter ;* and in fact we find that it corresponds much more closely than the present Reformed Dutch Liturgy with an interesting description of the services of the Walloon congregation at London, given by a writer of the seventeenth century.†

The first edition of the Palatinate Liturgy is not extant. The second, published in 1585,‡ has not been materially altered in subsequent reprints.

* The substance of A'Lasco's work was drawn, as shown in the preceding chapter, from Calvin's Liturgy of Strasburg. Thus it seems probable that we have here in the Palatinate Liturgy a nearer approach to that yet undiscovered document, than is afforded either by the Dutch or the Genevan formulary.

† Quoted by T. D. W., in the *Chr. Intell.* Some of those practices of ecclesiastical discipline which were recommended by Calvin, though not introduced successfully at Geneva, seem to have been followed out by the Palatinate Reformers. "It was lately enacted at Heidelberg," writes the Zurich theologian Gualter to Bishop Sandys, in 1573, "that no one should be admitted to the LORD'S Supper without having first presented himself to his pastor."—ZURICH LETTERS, clxxxvii : Parker Society.

‡ "Frederick III., elector Palatinate, in the year 1560, substituted the followers of Calvin's doctrines in place of the Lutheran teachers, whom he displaced, and ordered his subjects to receive the rites and opinions of the Genevans. His successor Lewis, in the year 1576, rescinded the acts of his father, and restored the Lutheran doctrine. But this again fell on the accession of John Casimir in 1583. From that time onward, the Palatinate Church held the second rank among the Reformed Churches ; and it possessed such influence over the others, that the religious instructions composed for its use by Ursinus, and denominated the Heidelberg Catechism, were received nearly throughout the whole body."—MOSHEIM, vol. iii. p. 384.

The same formulary was adopted by the general Synod of the Lower Rhine.* How generally it is in use at the present day, we are not informed.

The order of Divine service for the Lord's day in the morning, according to the Palatinate Liturgy, is as follows :—

GENERAL INTRODUCTION.

Grace, mercy, and peace, from God our Father, and his Beloved Son Jesus Christ our Lord, and the fellowship of the Holy Ghost, be with us all. *Amen.*

or,

The grace of the Lord Jesus Christ, and the love of God, and the communion of the Holy Ghost, be with you all. *Amen.*

EXHORTATION TO PRAYER.

To be used occasionally by the minister before the Sermon, especially on week-days.

Beloved in the Lord Jesus Christ : Let us call upon our faithful God and Father, and humbly beseech him to turn away his face from our sins, by which we have continually kindled his wrath against us. And whereas we are

* Ebrard, p. 30.

altogether unworthy to appear before his Holy Majesty, let us entreat him to look upon us in the face of his beloved Son JESUS CHRIST our LORD, accept of the merits of his sufferings and death in satisfaction for all our sins, and thus render us acceptable unto him.   Let us also supplicate him that he would by his HOLY SPIRIT enlighten us with the right understanding of his word, and grant us grace to receive the same with true faith and humility; that we may learn therefrom to withdraw all our confidence from creatures, and trust in him alone, to serve and glorify him. That so our whole lives may praise his name; and that seeing he hath been pleased to call and accept of us as his servants and children, and heirs of future glory, we may render him that love and obedience which faithful children owe unto their Father, and servants to their Lord. Let us therefore beseech him for these things, as our gracious Lord and Saviour JESUS CHRIST hath taught us to pray, sincerely saying:—OUR FATHER, etc.*

[*Then a Psalm is sung by the congregation.*]

* This exhortation is derived word for word from Calvin, who used it as a " bidding prayer" in his daily lectures. We have given it in a precatory form in Sec. III.: see page 66.

Q

PRAYER BEFORE SERMON.

Heavenly Father, eternal and merciful GOD: We acknowledge and confess before thy Divine Majesty that we are poor miserable sinners, conceived and born in sin and corruption, prone to all evil, and unfit for any good. By our sinful life, we have continually transgressed thy holy commandments, provoked thy wrath against us, and incurred thy just judgment unto eternal death. But, O LORD, we repent in sorrow that we have thus offended thee, we condemn ourselves and our iniquities, and implore thee mercifully to help us in our wretchedness and woe. Have mercy upon us, therefore, O most gracious GOD and Father, and pardon all our sins, for the sake of the holy sufferings of thy dear Son, JESUS CHRIST our Lord.

And vouchsafe unto us, henceforth, the grace of thy HOLY SPIRIT; that he may teach us heartily to know our unrighteousness, and make us so to abhor ourselves: that sin may be slain in us, and we may arise to newness of life. Thus shall we produce the perfect fruits of holiness and righteousness with which, for CHRIST'S sake, thou art well pleased. Grant also, that we may rightly understand thy holy word, according to thy Divine will, that we may learn from thence to withdraw our confidence entirely from the creature, and to put all our trust in thee. And may our old man, with all his lusts, be daily crucified more and more; that we may present ourselves unto thee, as living sacrifices, to the honour of thy holy name, the edification of each other, and the furtherance of our salvation: Through our Lord JESUS CHRIST, who hath also taught us to pray, saying :—OUR FATHER, etc.*

[Here follows the Sermon.]

On Sabbaths after the Morning Sermon, and especially after the preparatory Sermon, the minister shall say:

Beloved in the Lord, Whereas we see in the commandments of GOD, as in a glass, how great and manifold our sins are, by which we merit temporal and eternal punishment: therefore let each one of us heartily confess the same unto our faithful Father, and sincerely say with me:

* From Calvin: compare with the Liturgy of Geneva.

CONFESSION OF SIN.

I poor sinner, acknowledge before thee, my GOD and Creator, that I have grievously and in manifold ways sinned against thee, not only with gross outward transgressions, but much more with inward natural blindness, unbelief, doubts, despondency, impatience, pride, evil covetousness, secret envy, hatred, malice, and other sinful affections : as thou my Lord and GOD well knowest, and I, alas! cannot deeply enough deplore. But I repent of these things, and am sorry for them, and heartily beseech thee for mercy, for the sake of thy beloved Son JESUS CHRIST. Amen.*

Then shall the minister declare unto penitent believers the forgiveness of sins, and unto the impenitent the judgment of God, and say :

DECLARATION OF GRACE.

Hearken now unto the comforting assurance of the grace of GOD, promised in the Gospel to all that believe.

---

* This confession is of Lutheran origin; we meet with it in all the German Liturgies.   The interpolation was doubtless made during the brief period of the ascendancy of Lutheranism at Heidelberg, mentioned in the note on page 223.

Thus saith our Lord JESUS CHRIST : For GOD so loved the world, that he gave his only begotten Son, that whosoever believeth in him might not perish, but have everlasting life.

Unto as many of you therefore, beloved Brethren, as abhor yourselves and your sins, and believe that you are fully pardoned through the merits of JESUS CHRIST, and resolve daily more to abstain therefrom and to serve the LORD in true holiness and righteousness : I declare, according to the command of GOD, that they are released in heaven from all their sins, (as he hath promised in his Gospel,) through the perfect satisfaction of the most holy passion and death of our Lord JESUS CHRIST.

But as there may be some among you, who continue to find pleasure in your sin and shame, or who persist in sin against their conscience, I declare unto such, by the command of GOD, that the wrath and judgment of GOD abides upon them, and that all their sins are retained in heaven, and finally that they can never be delivered from eternal damnation, unless they repent.

And inasmuch as we doubt not that our prayers are sanctified by the sufferings of JESUS CHRIST, and therefore acceptable to GOD, let us heartily call upon him, and say :—OUR FATHER, etc.*

PRAYER AFTER THE MORNING SERMON.

Almighty GOD, Creator of heaven and earth, we give thee most hearty thanks, that thou hast created us, and hast preserved, fed, and sustained us and our children hitherto, and art still willing to keep and govern us. But especially do we thank thee that thou hast given us to know thy Son JESUS CHRIST, and dost pardon our sins for the sake of his bitter passion and death.

We beseech thee to renew us in the image of thy Son JESUS CHRIST, by the preaching of thy word, and the power of the HOLY GHOST, that so we may, both in soul and body, live with thee, to praise thee, for which we were created. Defend us against the malice of Satan, lest he pluck thy holy word out of our hearts, as he did unto our first parents Adam and Eve.

And whereas thou hast ordained civil authorities, by which thou dost govern us, we beseech thee,

---

* Here we have the "Declaration of Pardon" from A'Lasco, (and possibly from Calvin,) described by a Dutch author of the seventeenth century as used in the Walloon Church at London. According to his description, the recital of the Creed followed upon this declaration.

who hast the hearts of rulers in thy hands, for
* * * * Grant unto our governors grace and
peace, that they may direct their authority to the
end, that our Lord JESUS CHRIST, unto whom all
power in heaven and earth is given, may reign
over them and their subjects : so that this people,
who are the creatures of thy hands, and the sheep
of thy pasture, and for whom the LORD JESUS
shed his blood, may be governed in holiness and
righteousness ; and that we may, for thy sake,
show unto them all becoming honour and faithfulness, and thus, under their protection, lead an
honest, peaceable, and Christian life.

Grant thy blessing and favour also upon the
fruits of the earth, that we may thus know thee as
our Father, and the fountain of all mercy and
blessing.   Preserve us also from war, famine, and
the swift-spreading pestilence.   Neither pray we
for ourselves alone, but for all men in the whole
world, that thou wouldst graciously have compassion upon them.   And especially for those who
have fellowship with us in the Body of JESUS
CHRIST, and who suffer for the Truth's sake.   Be
pleased, O Father of all grace, to restrain the
wrath of thine enemies, who persecute thy Son
JESUS CHRIST in his members ; and strengthen

the persecuted with victorious steadfastness, and the power of thy HOLY SPIRIT, that they may joyfully receive these sufferings from thy hand, and in the midst of tribulations experience that peace which passeth all understanding.

Comfort and sustain the poor, the sick, widows and orphans, all prisoners, and such as are with child, together with all troubled and tempted souls, and grant unto them thy peace, through our Lord JESUS CHRIST, according to his assured promise : Verily, verily, I say unto you, all things that ye shall ask the Father in my name, will he give unto you; and who hath farther instructed us to pray :—OUR FATHER, etc.

After the Prayer a short Psalm may be sung, and the congregation dismissed to their homes with the

BENEDICTION.

The LORD bless thee, and keep thee. The LORD make his face shine upon thee, and be gracious unto thee. The Lord lift up his countenance upon thee, and give thee peace. *Amen.*

XIII.

The Directory of Worship Revised.

"It has even occurred to me to doubt, whether the well-known doctrine of our beloved Church, with regard to Liturgies, may not have been so rigidly interpreted, and so unskilfully applied, as to lead to practical misapprehension and mischief in regard to the devotional part of the services of our sanctuaries."

MILLER ON PUBLIC PRAYER.

IT was at the close of the American Revolution, when the various denominations of Christians in this country occupied themselves with a re-construction of their various ecclesiastical systems, that our Church, like others, revised her standards, and brought them to their present substance and shape. And the fact is not a little worthy of remark, that in the process of this revision, an effort was made by some of the most prominent men of our denomination, to introduce, as a modification of the directory of worship, a collection of *devotional forms ;* based on the same general principles, but presenting a liturgical aspect, and possessing many features of originality and interest.

Let us briefly state the circumstances under which this attempt was made. In 1786, the Synod of New York and Philadelphia appointed a Committee to modify and arrange the book of government and discipline, and adapt it to the use of the Church under the new civil dispensation.* Another Committee was appointed to perform a similar work in respect to the Directory of Worship: it consisted of the Rev. Drs. John Rodgers and MacWhorter, and the Rev. Messrs. Alexander Miller and James Wilson. The same individuals were directed to print the draught of the form of government and discipline. The whole appeared in 1787, in the shape of a pamphlet of one hundred and forty-three pages; of which the copy we have consulted is, perhaps, the only one extant.†

In this document, the various parts of public prayer, instead of being made the subject of directions as to the manner of conducting them, are provided for in liturgical forms. Such was the arrangement under which the Committee appointed

---

* HODGE's *History of the Pres. Church in the U. S.*, pt. ii. p. 498.

† A DRAUGHT *of the Form of the Government and Discipline* [and of the Directory of Worship] *of the Presbyterian Church in the United States of America.* New York: Printed by S. and J. London, No. 5, Water-street, MDCCLXXXVII. 143 pp. 8vo.

to revise the Directory returned it for the Synod's adoption. They judged that, for the ministrations of the Sanctuary, it were better to provide samples than recipes; specimens of what these services ought to be, rather than descriptions of the mode of making them.

When the Directory, thus altered, came up before the Synod for approval, and the question was raised, whether these forms should stand as they appeared on the draught—or whether the several parts and subjects of prayer should be stated as formerly, *in thesi*, that is, in a doctrinal form—a variety of opinions were expressed. The latter method was ultimately carried by a majority; but many, among whom was the late Dr. Green,* voted for a retention of the forms; on the ground, that an exemplification of any matter of instruction must be considered the best mode of making it intelligible and plain. Of course, the idea of a *confinement* to forms was entertained by no one.

These proposed changes in our Book of Worship, as they did not prevail at the time of their introduction, being rejected by a majority of votes, possess, of course, no authoritative value. Yet we

* *Memoir of the Rev.* DR. GREEN. New York, R. Carter: pp. 182, 184.

cannot regard them without interest; for they represent the views of some of the leading men of the Church at that period, and furnish an exemplification of the manner in which, according to their judgment, the Presbyterian order of worship may best be observed. They prove, also, that by the interpretation of competent minds, the principles of the Church do not conflict with the discretionary use of liturgical forms.

The preface to this interesting document expresses " high respect for the other Protestant Churches of this country, though several of them differ from" our communion " in some forms of government and modes of worship; particularly for the regular Congregational Churches to the eastward; for the Associate, Low Dutch, and German Reformed Churches; and for the Lutheran and Episcopal Churches. With any of the above denominations," it continues, " the people of the Presbyterian Church are recommended to worship where there is no regular service of their own."

Such courtesies of denominational intercourse seem to have been quite in vogue during the early years of our national existence. Having suffered in common the evils of war and disorder, " the different religious denominations of Christians," to use the language of the Preface to the Common Prayer Book, " were left at full and equal liberty to model and organize their respective Churches, and forms of worship and discipline, in such manner as they might judge most convenient for their future prosperity." And they went about this work in a spirit of kindliness and fraternity towards one another. It may be doubted whether time and growth have improved the temper of ecclesiastical bodies, or even maintained as liberal and conciliatory a spirit.

The Preface goes on to recommend " greater regularity in reading the Scriptures as a part of public worship;" and advises as " decent, and not improper, for the whole congregation to stand up during the reading of the Scriptures ; as was the usage under the Old Testament dispensation, and among the primitive Christians."

To show the nature of the forms contained in this work, we shall select some portions of them, and begin with the

SERVICE FOR THE LORD'S DAY MORNING.

" After the congregation is assembled, the minister shall begin the service with prayer, to the following purpose :

" HOLY, holy, holy, LORD GOD Almighty! who art, and wast, and art to come. We, who are unworthy of the least of all thy mercies, humbly present ourselves in thy courts. We come to thee our Creator and Redeemer, with homage, adoration, and praise. Enable us, O LORD! by thy good Spirit, to attend to the holy duties to which thou art calling us at this time, without distraction of mind, and with reverence and godly fear. Admit us, we beseech thee, with humble boldness to enter into the holiest, by the blood of JESUS, by the new and living way which he hath consecrated for us through the vail. Instruct us from thy word. May we read it with wise and understanding hearts. Prepare us for singing thy praises: may we make melody in our hearts, and offer up an acceptable service. Teach us to pray; inspire us with a spirit of devotion; enable us to exercise faith in all the parts of Divine worship. And let all be done to the glory of the Father, and of the Son, and of the Holy Ghost; and graciously accept us, through JESUS CHRIST our Lord. Amen."

" This, and all the other prayers in the Directory, may and ought to be varied, according to the variety of circumstances which may occur, agreeably to the views and judgment of every minister. Thus the spirit of prayer will be encouraged, and the undue restraint of this spirit, which is the too frequent effect of forms of prayer, will be guarded against."

The Prayer before Sermon is too long for transcription in this place. It was evidently designed rather to supply matter of selection, than for use as a whole.

The direction at the close reads thus :—

" As the prayer which CHRIST taught his disciples is both a pattern for prayer, and itself a most comprehensive prayer, we recommend it to be used in the prayers of the Church; and we think the most proper place for this purpose is, either at the conclusion of the introductory prayer, or at the end of this."*

Would that this counsel of our fathers might be heard and regarded throughout our churches! Then should we not listen in vain from year to year for the utterance of those blessed words in our pulpits, which in the closet are so precious to every believer.

---

* This paragraph was not new in the Draught of 1787, but was taken, word for word, from the old Directory. For what reason it came to be omitted in our present formulary, we cannot conjecture.

ADMINISTRATION OF BAPTISM.

We pass on to the service for the administration of Baptism. The Invocation at the beginning of this service reads as follows:—

" Most merciful GOD! we pray for thy blessing upon these parents and their child. The souls of parents and of children are thine own. Enable these parents, with faith and love, to offer up their child to thee, in this holy ordinance of baptism. Sanctify this child by thy grace. May his original guilt be done away, through the blood of the Lamb that was slain. Wash this child in the laver of regeneration. Ingraft him into CHRIST, and make him an heir of glory. Join the inward baptism of the SPIRIT with the outward baptism of water. Graciously bless and sanctify this holy ordinance to the spiritual benefit of this child. Ratify in heaven what we now do on earth. Hear us, O our GOD! accept and answer us, only for the sake of our Divine Redeemer. Amen.

" Then the minister, either taking the child in his arms, or leaving it in the arms of the parent, shall call the child by its name," and so proceed with the rite of baptism.

"This being performed, he shall pray to this or the like purpose:

"O Thou most glorious, condescending, and gracious God! Father, Son, and Holy Ghost: We give thee hearty thanks for the covenant of thy grace, and for all the institutions of thy mercy. Follow with thy blessing this holy ordinance of baptism, which has now been administered in thy name. Enable these parents to live in the faithful discharge of every Christian duty toward this child. Receive him into thy Fatherly care and protection. May he live and grow up before thee, and do worthily in his day and generation. Sanctify him by thy Spirit; uphold him by thy power. May he prove a useful member of thy Church here, and be kept by faith unto salvation: Through JESUS CHRIST our Lord. Amen."

ADMINISTRATION OF THE LORD'S SUPPER.

Our third selection shall be from the service for the administration of the LORD's Supper. The prayer before the distribution of the elements is prefaced thus:—

"Let the minister take a portion of the bread in one hand, and one of the cups in the other, and then pray for a blessing, to this or the like effect:

"O thou Eternal GOD! Father, Son, and Holy Spirit: We adore thee as the fountain of being and blessedness. We praise thee that thou hast formed a Church in this fallen world; that we are called to be members of it; and that thou hast appointed various ordinances to be observed therein. And now, LORD! we are invited to come and eat of Wisdom's bread, and to drink of the wine that thou hast mingled. Cause us to hunger and thirst after righteousness, that we may be filled. Draw us, and we will run after thee. Bring us unto thy presence, that we may be glad and rejoice in thee, and remember thy love more than wine.

"Most gracious GOD! we give thee glory for all the purposes of thy love; for the mission, sufferings, and death of JESUS CHRIST; in whose name alone we have access to the throne of thy grace, and hope for everlasting life. We thank thee for this holy ordinance. We devoutly pray for thy blessing upon us, in our attendance at this feast of love.

"Bless, O LORD! these elements of bread and wine. May we receive them as the symbols of the broken body and shed blood of our Lord and Saviour JESUS CHRIST.   May we by faith eat the flesh and drink the blood of the Son of GOD.   Let the cup of blessing which we bless, be to us the communion of the blood of CHRIST; let this bread which we break, be to us the communion of the body of CHRIST.

"Most merciful Father! keep our hearts and minds in this solemn duty; and preserve us from the suggestions of the evil one.   May our souls feel the lively exercise of every grace.   Join us to thee in a new and everlasting covenant, and make us one spirit with thyself.   May thy continual grace further and assist us in the performance of every duty of the Christian life.   Seal unto us the remission of all our sins, the gift of the Holy Ghost, and the promise of eternal life.

"And now unto Him that is able to keep us from falling, and to present us faultless before the presence of his glory with exceeding joy: To the only wise GOD our Saviour, be glory and majesty, dominion and power, both now and for ever. Amen."

FORM OF ADMISSION TO THE CHURCH.

A subject in which our present directory of worship leaves much to be desired, is the "Admission of Persons to Sealing Ordinances of the Church." The want of any provision for that service, has been generally remedied among us by the adoption of voluntary and extraneous forms, such as are in use among our Congregational brethren. This deficiency the Draught of 1787 admirably supplies. We quote it at some length.

The Form of Admission to the Church is introduced with these observations :—

" Those who are to be admitted to sealing ordinances, shall be examined as to their knowledge and belief of the following things :

" That the Scriptures of the Old and New Testaments are the word of GOD, the only infallible rule of faith and practice.

" That these contain, sufficiently and plainly, every doctrine needful for salvation.

" That there is one only living and true GOD, possessed of every perfection and excellency : Creator, Preserver, and Governor of the universe.

"That there are three Persons in the GOD-HEAD: the Father, the Son, and the Holy Spirit; and that these three are one.

"That all men are in a lost estate, and, as sinners, stand justly condemned by the law of GOD, and are liable to his wrath and curse.

"That JESUS CHRIST, the only begotten Son of GOD, who is GOD and man in one Person, came into this world to seek and to save them that are lost.

"That He suffered and made atonement in their room and stead.

"That He died for their offences, and rose again for their justification.

"That He sitteth at the right hand of GOD in heaven, making continual intercession for them.

"That the enlightening and sanctifying influences of the HOLY GHOST are absolutely necessary to lead us into the saving understanding of the Sacred Scriptures; to renew the heart; and to enable a Christian to live godly in the world. And that watchfulness over the life, holy meditation, a conscientious attendance upon public, private, and secret worship; together with the steady practice of righteousness, truth, sincerity, and charity toward men, and of sobriety, chastity, and temperance toward ourselves; are the indispensable duties of every Christian.

" When the knowledge of those who are to be admitted to sealing ordinances is judged to be satisfactory, and nothing appears in their life and conversation to hinder their admission, the minister shall, either in private, or in the presence of the Session, or in the presence of the congregation, as shall be most expedient, ask the profession of their faith, in the following or like manner:

" Do you believe JESUS CHRIST to be the Son of GOD? Do you assent to the covenant of grace, and acknowledge the obligation of your baptismal engagements? Do you take GOD, the Father, Son, and Holy Ghost, to be your GOD? Do you renounce your former sins? And do you promise, through grace, to live in the diligent practice of all the duties required in the Gospel?

" It is not improper that this be accompanied with suitable exhortation and prayer. And the persons so professing their faith are, immediately thereupon, entitled to sealing ordinances.

" Unbaptized persons are not members of the visible Church—they are not Christians: Therefore, when they offer themselves, they are to be considered as candidates for admission into the Church, and are to be taught the doctrines of the Gospel as above directed.

" When their knowledge shall be deemed satisfactory, and nothing appears in their life against their admission, it is most expedient, in ordinary cases, that they should publicly profess their faith, in the presence of the congregation [in the same or like manner as directed above in the admission of young Christians to sealing ordinances]: after which they ought to be immediately baptized, and admitted to all the privileges of the Church."

MARRIAGE SERVICE.

We close these quotations with the two prayers of the Marriage Service, which in other respects is similar to that of our Directory. The Invocation reads as follows:—

" Most holy and gracious GOD! Maker of our bodies, and Father of our spirits : We praise thee that thou hast made us rational creatures, capable of enjoying the various blessings of the social life. We thank thee for the institution of Marriage ; and that thou hast made it honourable in all. Be pleased to bless these persons who are about to be joined in this holy relation. May they, being united to each other in the marriage covenant, be united to the LORD JESUS in that covenant which is ordered in all things and sure. Enable them to enter on this important relation in the fear of the LORD; having abundant cause to rejoice in that providence which hath formed it between them. We pray for thy gracious presence with us; the pardon of our sins; and the acceptance of our persons and our services: For the sake of JESUS CHRIST thy Son, our only LORD and SAVIOUR. Amen."

The concluding prayer reads thus:

"Most merciful GOD! in whom all the families of the earth are blessed: We pray for thy favour to descend on these persons, whom now, in thy holy providence, thou hast brought into the marriage relation. Bless them with all spiritual and temporal benedictions. May they dwell together in love, as joint heirs of the grace of life, that their prayers be not hindered. To thine indulgent providence, O LORD! we commit them, beseeching thee that goodness and mercy may follow them all the days of their life. We thank thee for this joyful occasion; and that the voice of the bridegroom and of the bride is still heard in the land. May we rejoice in thy fear. Keep us from sin. Pardon all our transgressions. Help us to live faithful to the duties of our various relations. Guide us by thy counsel through this world: and afterwards receive us to glory. And now unto the Father, and the Son, and the Holy Ghost, be ascribed endless praises. Amen."

Such was the character of the liturgical preparation submitted to the Synod of 1787, as a substitute for the Directory of Worship. Its rejection does not seem to have been based upon the ground of its liturgical form, as foreign to the spirit of the Church; but proceeded, we may suppose, from an unwillingness to alter to such an extent any of the existing standards, which were only modified so far as the conditions of the times demanded. It does not appear that any discussion took place on the subject. It was dropped; and the previous method of providing for religious worship was recurred to.

The bearing of these facts upon the lawfulness of a discretionary use of liturgies in the Presbyterian Church, will hardly require indication. The men who composed these forms of worship for the edification of the Church, were probably unacquainted with what had been done ages before in the same direction. The Liturgies of Calvin and Knox had remained unknown for a century and more, beyond the range, perhaps, of occasional antiquarian researches. It was, therefore, no imitation of obsolete customs that prompted our American Divines in drawing up this formulary; but a wise and judicious interpretation of the laws and the spirit of Presbyterianism itself.

XIV.

Conclusion.

"It is not, surely, because we think that prayers are nowhere to be had but at Rome? That were a foul scorn and indignity cast upon all the Reformed Churches and our own:—If we imagine that all the godly ministers of England are not able to new mould a better and more pious Liturgy than this, which was conceived and infanted by an idolatrous mother."—MILTON.

THE facts elicited in the course of these inquiries will, we apprehend, readily satisfy any mind, that our Church possesses a devotional literature of her own, rich and copious.

What practical suggestions may arise from the review here taken, need not now be stated at any great length. They are such as will enter largely into the discussion of the whole subject of public worship, a discussion which is already commencing, and for which the times are ripe.

It is widely becoming manifest to our Churches, that comeliness and decorum in the house of GOD are not less worthy to be sought, than in the habitations of men; that a reverent approach to the Divine Majesty, and a careful choice of language in addressing the throne of grace, are proper matters of study; and may command, at least, the same solicitude that might be given to the forms of expression employed in addressing the great and honoured among men.

The experiment of that mode of dealing with the subject of Public Worship, by which everything is left to the unaided individuality of the minister, has been fully tried. For nearly two centuries, in the face of all historic precedent, at variance with all other denominations of Christians, and in conflict with their own earlier principles and practice, the Calvinistic Churches of Great Britain and the United States have faithfully adhered to this method, unknown in ecclesiastical experience before the sittings of the Westminster Assembly. We believe that the times are drawing near, when by general attestation that method will be pronounced defective.

No candid person, familiar with the actual condition of our churches, can refuse to confront this fact: That by so much as the Public Worship of GOD may be rendered attractive; may awaken interest, and excite and sustain devotional feeling; by so much have we lost power and influence as a Church. We conceive it to be plain beyond denial, that while the earnest and practical piety

of its members, the learning, ability, and fidelity
of its clergy, obtain for Presbyterianism a com-
manding position of respect and influence; the
effect of its external modes of worship, as at
present generally conducted, is rather to impair
than to augment the force of these advantages.
Evidently, the young are not drawn into our congregations by any beauty or impressiveness of
our services; their attachment is not won and
strengthened by interest in the devotional exercises
of the sanctuary. In a word, it is nothing else
than the power of preaching that brings men and
holds them to the bosom of our Church.

Would we exchange this state of things for its
reverse? Would we relinquish the spirit for the
form; and choose instead of an active and living
membership, and an able and faithful clergy, with
all external irregularities and imperfections, the
beautiful but soulless corpse of formalism? As-
suredly, no! Yet this consideration does not reconcile us to existing defects, nor to the retention
of them when fairly experienced and palpably
exposed. The fact that they are comparatively
unessential, and merely superficial, augments the
urgency of an immediate redress.

As we started, however, upon a discussion

purely historical, so we limit our conclusions as to the results of these inquiries. Example, we have seen, abundantly warrants the use of liturgical forms in the Presbyterian Church. History gives forth but one utterance on the subject. Wherever Protestant Communions have been established, the institution of worship has been secured by formularies, in whose production the most able minds to be enlisted have been employed.

The Calvinistic Churches constitute no exception to this general rule. Those primitive Christians of the Alpine Valleys, the Waldenses, from time immemorial possessed and used a liturgical form. The Genevan Church was early favoured with a correct and well-conceived order of worship ; and that order was adopted in succession by all the national Presbyterian Churches of kindred faith and discipline. France, Scotland, Switzerland, Holland, Hungary,* Western Germany, almost at the same period, embraced this mode of

---

* EBRARD, whose statements are generally so reliable, ignores entirely the existence of a Liturgy in the Hungarian Church ; as indeed he seems quite unacquainted with that of Scotland. But the historian LAMPE speaks distinctly of such a ritual in use among the Hungarian Churches of the Reformed or Calvinistic order ; and quotes largely from a "Liturgy of the Lord's Supper" published at Saros-Patak in 1658. He gives a full description of the mode of celebrating the Communion ; which seems to have closely resembled

worship. It was long before even the Independents of England relinquished its use. To this day, Great Britain and America offer the sole instances of Calvinistic Churches without a Liturgy.

But we shall doubtless be called upon to account for the total abandonment of these forms in Scotland, where they were established at so early a period, and sanctioned by repeated ecclesiastical enactments. If truly consonant with our system of faith and practice, why has the liturgical element there so utterly disappeared; leaving only a violent hostility to everything that savours of a liturgical nature? The feeling which has long prevailed in Scotland on this subject, though now happily softening, is evidently the traditional consequence of events long past, but vividly remembered by the popular mind. "It has arisen," says a Scottish writer, "out of the fearful evils and abuses flowing from the shameless and idolatrous forms of Popery, mumbled

that of the Strasburg Church. The order is as follows : 1. Exhortation. 2. Confession of Sins. 3. The Creed. 4. Absolution. 5. Singing of a Psalm. 6. Recital of the words of the Institution. 7. Participation, during which Psalms are sung. 8. Closing Address. 9. Thanksgiving, and Benediction.—LAMPE, *Hist. Eccles. Hungar.*, Appendix.

over by a lazy and corrupt priesthood, without feeling, and almost without decency; succeeded by the cruel and insane attempts to force upon a reluctant people forms containing sentiments and rites which they abhorred." *   "This morbid terror for everything approaching to form," says another, "grew partly out of the unjustifiable efforts of Laud and his master to force a justly obnoxious Liturgy on a free people." † The feeling is undoubtedly beginning to give way to a more enlightened and Christian appreciation of the intrinsic merits of the question, viewed apart from prejudices which ought long since to have been buried and forgotten.

We have been led to regard it as in some sense a providential indication, that while completing these sketches and studies, which have occupied the leisure moments of a succession of years, we have seen springing up in various quarters the first signs of interest respecting a matter so long and so utterly neglected. Religious journals, whose indignant frown would a few months since

* The Editor of the volume entitled " *Family Worship; a Series of Prayers, by* 180 *Clergymen of the Church of Scotland,*" Glasgow, 1841; Preface, p. v.

† From an article on John Knox's Liturgy, in the Edinburgh Review, April, 1852.

have repelled the mooting of certain questions, are now engaged in their serious and attentive consideration. Ecclesiastical bodies in correspondence with our own, have begun to take action upon the revival of their ancient forms of worship, hitherto regarded with indifference.* Prominent divines are expressing, though privately and cautiously, views which as yet they do not venture to carry into practice.

We cannot refer these facts to a growth of formalism. Those who take ground against us, will undoubtedly find it their easiest method to dispose of the subject by such a reference. But so far as we can trace the desire now manifesting itself for a

---

* We allude to the Dutch and German Reformed Churches; both of them Calvinistic as respects their doctrine, and Presbyterian in order and discipline.

We may add, that the Presbyterian Church of Scotland took a step in this direction, when in 1849 the General Assembly appointed a Committee to prepare a Book of Devotion, with a series of Scriptural lessons, for the use of colonists and seamen. This is certainly an important measure; and it may be questioned, whether a wise policy would not lead our own Assembly to order the preparation of such a manual. Few of us are aware of the loss already resulting from the want of a formulary of this nature, suitable for use in the army and navy of the United States. We have heard the remark from a Presbyterian layman who stands high in the political world, that this deficiency is contributing to the rapid spread of Episcopalianism among the officers and men of both army and navy; so much so that the day may be looked for when that denomination will embrace the entire military force of our country.

more decent celebration of the rites and ordinances of religion, it proceeds from an honest and well-founded conviction, that in departing from the early practice of our Church, we have greatly lost sight of the correct principles and the proper ends of religious worship; and thus have failed to do a great work for the honour of GOD and the edification of his people.

"There is, in this country," says a Scottish author already quoted, "what we cannot but consider a very unreasonable prejudice against the use of forms in all circumstances. Yet it is a well-known fact that our early Reformers prepared and used forms in the worship of GOD. * * * We need not refer to the form left us by our LORD as an example of such a practice; where his disciples were taught to '*say*' the same words. Indeed, what are all the passages of Scripture usually adopted in extempore prayer? What are the Apostolic Benedictions, but forms of prayer?"*

Such language, from such a source, indicates surely the commencement of a more enlightened feeling on the subject in the Church of Scotland.

* *Family Worship of the Church of Scotland*, Preface, p. v.

Of this, indeed, we have elsewhere sufficient evidence. The translators of Calvin's works, now in course of publication at Edinburgh, introduce the Liturgy of that Reformer as " possessing a considerable degree of interest; both as exhibiting the Form of Church Service which, under his auspices, was adopted at Geneva, and also as containing at least *the germ* of what still appears to some *a very important desideratum*—a regular Form of Public Worship, with such a degree of latitude in the use of it as leaves full scope for ministerial freedom."*

To the same effect is the opinion expressed by a prominent lay-member of the Scottish Church, the present Duke of Argyle. Attributing the alienation of so many of the leading families of Scotland from her Church, he does not hesitate to say: " A partial use of liturgical forms of prayer, to which the first Scottish Reformers had no objection, and which the legislative institutions of Presbytery entitle it to adopt at any moment, would alone, I think, have been of immense value in engaging the affections, and preventing the straying of its members."†

* CALVIN'S TRACTS, Edinburgh, 1849; Preface, p. xiv.
† JOHN KNOX'S *Liturgy*, etc., Edinburgh Review, April, 1852.

The views of the Rev. Dr. Cumming, the distinguished minister of the Scottish Church in London, are well known. "For the great mass of the clergy," he says, "I believe that the partial use of a form of prayer would be truly valuable." And again: "I believe that the resumption—if the word may be used of that which is not rescinded—of the Liturgy I now edit, by the Church of Scotland, and by authority of the Ecclesiastical Courts, would be attended with great good. It could by no possibility do mischief. Even if it should not find its way to the approval and adoption of those who are more prominent in character and powerful in influence, in the General Assembly of the Scottish Church, it may be of great service as a model of spiritual, scriptural, and truly solemn Church Service for every clergyman."*

An able article in the Edinburgh Review, for April, 1852, concludes an examination of the Liturgies of the Reformers, with the following remarks: "Of the opinions of individuals, so long as those opinions are not publicly expressed, we are not entitled publicly to speak: but thus much we may say, that we have good grounds for thinking that the views which we have pro-

* Preface to an edition of KNOX's *Liturgy*, London, 1840, pp. vii., ix.

pounded are neither new nor strange to many of the more liberal, and some of the most influential ministers of the Church of Scotland. Dr. Cumming fired no random shot when he said, in speaking of the combination of formal and extempore prayer in Knox's Liturgy, ' This arrangement would have conciliated the great bulk of the Scottish clergy in the seventeenth century, and I believe *would be generally acceptable in the nineteenth.*' If the clergy and people of Scotland could once be satisfied (and we see no reason why they should not) that formal prayer would never be allowed to transgress the limits which Coleridge has assigned to ceremonies generally, viz.: of ' pure glass to see Heaven through, not dyed in the gorgeous crimsons and purple, blue and green of the drapery of saints and saintesses,' then we believe it might be re-introduced, with an universality of consent, that would silence the tongue of even Jenny Geddes herself."*

We look for no ecclesiastical enactments in America, to bring about the desired improvement in our forms of public worship. But there are certain measures which in strict conformity with existing laws, and in the faithful following out of

* JOHN KNOX's *Liturgy*, Edinburgh Review, April, 1852.

acknowledged principles, we may hope to see widely adopted toward this end. These measures we shall classify under two heads,—immediate and ultimate.

Of immediate practicability, and of primary importance, are:—First, the resumed use of those ancient, Scriptural, and Apostolic Elements of Worship; those forms which as much belong to our service as the Benediction with which it closes; forms which not without intent are appended to our authorized standards,* as they are also enjoined upon our children for frequent rehearsal:† we speak of the Lord's Prayer, the Ten Commandments, and the Apostles' Creed. It is no slight error of our churches to have abandoned so generally these forms, the basis of our denominational order of worship.‡ As there can be no question of the propriety, so we have little doubt as to the possibility of at once recurring to their use.§

* _Constitution of the Presbyterian Church in the United States_, pp. 397—399; after the Shorter Catechism.

† _Directory for Worship_, c. ix.

‡ This is more true of our own country than of Scotland; where we are told it is not uncommon to hear the Decalogue and the Lord's Prayer repeated in Divine service.

§ The proper location of these forms in our service for the Morning of the Lord's Day, is: _The Lord's Prayer_, at the close of the first

The second step which we regard as practicable and important at the present moment, is the regular and continuous reading of Holy Scripture, at every religious service, and in sufficient portions. The prevailing neglect of this part of Divine worship, it is difficult to account for; especially when taking into view the repeated and distinct injunctions of our Church on the subject.* There

Prayer, or Invocation. *The Ten Commandments*, after the Invocation and LORD's Prayer. *The Creed*, at the end of the second or "long prayer;" prefaced with a short petition, like that on p. 43, or p. 70. It will be observed that in the Calvinistic worship, the Creed is generally used as a prayer.

* The First Book of Discipline of the Church of Scotland, Anno 1560, speaks thus: "We think it most expedient that the Scripture be read in order; that is, that some one Book of the Old and New Testament be begun and orderly read to the end. For this skipping and divagation from place to place of Scripture, be it in reading, or be it in preaching, we judge not so profitable to edify the Kirk, as the continual following of one text."—Ch. xi. DUNLOP's *Conf.*, ii. 585.

† The Directory for Public Worship, adopted by the Church of Scotland in 1645, orders: "How large a portion shall be read at once, is left to the wisdom of the minister; but it is convenient that ordinarily one chapter of each Testament be read at every meeting; and sometimes more, when the chapters be short, or the coherence of matter requireth it. It is requisite that all the canonical books be read over in order, that the people may be better acquainted with the whole body of the Scriptures; and, ordinarily, where the reading in either Testament endeth on one LORD's day, it is to begin the next."—*Of Public Reading of the Holy Scriptures.*

The American revision of the Directory modifies considerably the force of this regulation. Long neglect of the practice prescribed, led doubtless to this change in the letter of the law. Thus reads the American Directory: "The Holy Scriptures of the Old and New Testaments shall be publicly read, from the most approved translation are doubtless some ministers who habitually read one portion of Scripture at each service; and perhaps a few who adhere to the ancient rule of reading two selections, one from each Testament. But this is rare; and very commonly the duty is altogether omitted in the second or afternoon service. The fact is deeply to be deplored. The reading of Scripture is a constituent part of Divine worship. In the Temple and Synagogue it occupied a very considerable place. All Christian Churches, primitive and degenerate, have been unanimous in this custom. There can be no justification of its neglect; which has risen purely out of that strange disposition to slight whatever is regular and prescriptive in the rites of religion ; a radicalism that has destroyed the beauty of our Sanctuaries, and that finds no defence save in an invincible prejudice.*

in the vulgar tongue, that all may hear and understand. How large a portion shall be read at once, is left to the discretion of every minister; however, in each service, he ought to read, at least, one chapter; and more, when the chapters are short, or the connexion requires it."—Ch. iii.

* This unreasoning and unreasonable ultraism, which in Zurich of old excluded the use of vocal music, in Scotland now opposes the use of organs, and the reading of sermons, and in our own country objects to the wearing of the gown. Yet in Scotland and in Zurich the gown has always been worn, and in America the organ is used, and sermons are read without exciting displeasure.

A third measure proposed is a more strict adherence to the prescribed order of the Directory of
Worship.   The topics of prayer and their succes-
sions are clearly laid down in that formulary.
Without supplying the need of a Liturgy, it was
designed to prevent irregularity, and to secure
uniformity in the performance of public prayer.*
The rigid observance of that order, is incumbent
upon every minister who officiates in the Presbyterian Church.   Such an observance would at
least remove the more glaring objections to
unwritten prayer; wandering and diffuseness in
some portions, and in others the total omission of
important topics.†

In addition to these measures, there are others
which we hope to see ultimately prevail.   We look
for the time when our congregations shall take

---

* What the compilers of our Directory meant it to be, we may
learn from their own Preface: "Our meaning therein being only
that the general heads, the sense and scope of the prayers, and other
parts of public worship *being known to all*, there may be a consent of
all the churches in those things that contain the substance of the
service and the worship of GOD; and the ministers may be thereby
directed, in their administrations, *to keep like soundness of doctrine
and prayer*, and may if need be have some help and furniture."—
Compendium of Laws of the Church of Scotland, Part I. p. 280.

† Such as intercession for rulers and magistrates; a duty most
clearly enjoined by Scripture, which, nevertheless, is very generally
neglected among us at the present day.

part in the public prayers of the Church, by an audible *Amen* at the close of each prayer; and by the recital of the LORD's Prayer and the Creed after the minister. We hope, also, to see the want of a formulary of Public Prayer and the administration of ordinances supplied, by a compilation of the best forms of devotion which have been used in our Church and in other Churches; furnishing sufficient variety for voluntary selection. This should not be the work of a single individual, nor can it be well accomplished within a short term of years. The endeavours of all who are favourable to such a production should be combined, and the general wants of our clergy should be consulted. And while we have little expectation that such a formulary, however perfect, will ever be adopted as a standard of the Church, we see not why at some future period it may not be recognised and sanctioned as a lawful aid to those who may desire its use.